UNDERSTANDING ADHD MEDICATION FOR MEN, WOMEN AND CHILDREN

COMPLETE GUIDE TO MANAGING YOUR ADHD MEDICATION, ACKNOWLEDGING THE SIDE EFFECTS, EXPLORING ALTERNATIVES AND AVOIDING ADDICTION

DAN BANACHOWSKI

CONTENTS

INTRODUCTION

Medication without explanation is obscene. —Toni Cade Bambara

Up to 16% of children under the age of 18 have an attention deficit hyperactivity disorder—also known as ADHD—diagnosis (Centers for Disease Control and Prevention, 2021). Anywhere between 58 and 92% of diagnosed children with ADHD receive treatment of some kind, and up to 81% of those cases receive medication as their treatment option. I do not mean to shout a bunch of numbers at you right off the bat, but my point is that there are significant amounts of children with ADHD who both do and do not take medication to treat their ADHD.

The fact of the matter is that there are successful people with ADHD, and the status of their medication does not matter. You can be just as happy and thriving with medication as without, and it is all about finding what choice is right for you. That said, I know that that choice is not necessarily easy by any means. After all, why are you here? Maybe you want to continue taking your medication, but you are afraid of addiction. Perhaps you are on the fence or had a bad experience with medication before. Whatever your reason may be, I'm here to tell you that ADHD medication is nothing to be afraid of. After reading this book, you will be much more confident in your knowledge and use of ADHD medication.

I bet you have heard that before–that you can trust and remain confident in someone's knowledge–but let me tell you about myself and how I know that ADHD medication is not only safe but an effective and wonderful option for ADHD treatment as well. I was diagnosed with ADHD at a young age, taking medication for it from single digits to about the middle years of my childhood. After that, I stopped taking my medication, using it exclusively for major ordeals like exams in school. I stopped taking it because the dosage was so high that it began to control my mood, diet, and more. This is why I'm writing this book–to explain that ADHD medication is a terrific solution if handled properly. Starting out the way I did is bound to traumatize anyone, but after educating yourself with these resources, your journey with ADHD medication will sail much smoother. I also want people to understand that there are alternatives to ADHD medication if comfort still is not there.

Now, let me be clear–this book is not meant to serve as medical advice. I'm just an ordinary person like you who has had my fair share of experiences with ADHD medication, and I want to share those experiences with others. This is not meant to serve as medical advice, but a starting point or suggestion for things to discuss with your doctor. Listen to your body and your doctor above all.

Despite all there is to know about ADHD medication, at 33 years old and with the experience I have, I'd say I know a fair bit. Nearly 30 years of my life have been spent learning the things I'm going to share with you today, so that you do not have to spend 30 years or more of YOUR life on the same journey. You can have a better start or continuation of your experience with ADHD medication.

So, without further delay, let's get started with the learning process.

1

INTRODUCING ADDERALL

The oldest and strongest emotion of mankind is fear, and the oldest and strongest kind of fear is fear of the unknown. —H.P. Lovecraft

When I say the word 'Adderall' to someone, two typical reactions appear. Either the person is completely oblivious to what I'm talking about, or they react negatively due to a negative association with Adderall. Many people only know it as the "over prescribed ADHD drug" that does not work, but that is not the case at all.

For example, some people agree that Adderall is the best and only thing to ever work for them, going as far as to say that Adderall saved their life. One such person is Elizabeth Broadbent, who works as a writer for ADDitude Magazine. In one of her articles, Broadbent mentioned that Adderall was truly a game changer for her and her experience with ADHD (Broadbent, 2021). It all started with some evening narcolepsy she had been experiencing, and no doctor could find the cause. It didn't seem like anything was doing it, including other medication. One doctor prescribed her Adderall, both for her ADHD and to handle the narcolepsy.

Fortunately, the medication worked! Not just for her narcolepsy, though; Broadbent experienced so many other positive impacts as well. For the first time in her life, she felt normal all thanks to the new medication. The medication made her feel like she could get stuff done better than ever before, and it entirely eliminated her executive dysfunction. It made her more social and kinder to her family, truly rotating her life for the better. This is the experience that ADHD medication has most often when prescribed appropriately by a reliable doctor; it is a life changer, not a life ruiner. Understanding more about Adderall is necessary to help you get the full picture, but first we have to explore the condition that necessitates the medication itself.

WHAT IS ADHD?

ADHD is a very common disorder that primarily impacts the development of the brain (Centers for Disease Control and Prevention, 2022). For many people, it gets diagnosed during childhood, but ADHD is a lifelong disorder that does not disappear just because someone has grown older. On the contrary, ADHD persists and can even worsen in adulthood for some people. Primarily, ADHD impacts the ability to pay attention, control impulse behaviors, and remain sedentary when necessary.

ADHD presents itself in three different ways: Predominantly inattentive, predominantly hyperactive-impulsive, and combined presentation. In someone who has ADHD that has a predominantly inattentive presentation, it will be hard for them to focus, converse, or begin and end tasks. This type of ADHD is most common in adults and women, whereas hyperactive-impulsive presentation is more common in boys and children. For someone with ADHD that is predominantly hyperactive, they will struggle with sitting still. They might climb onto things, feel restless, speak out of turn, etc. as a result of their ADHD. And finally, we have combined presentation, wherein the two types of ADHD mentioned previously are in perfect balance.

We are not exactly sure what causes ADHD, but data shows that some things can reasonably be considered as causes of the condition. For example, brain anatomy and function play a role in the potential for someone to develop ADHD (American Academy of Pediatrics, 2019). This refers to a lower level of brain activity in certain areas of the brain that can lead to ADHD. Furthermore, studies have shown that genetics can play a role, as children from families with ADHD are more likely to develop ADHD themselves. Other potential causes for ADHD include head injury, prematurity, prenatal exposure to substances, and more. There is also significant data showing that there is no correlation between ADHD and diet, allergies, or vaccines.

ADHD medications work to alleviate the symptoms of ADHD, but they do not cure ADHD, nor should ADHD be considered something to be cured. It is not an illness; rather, it is simply a brain difference that contributes to human diversity. ADHD medication works for alleviating symptoms of the disorder by increasing the levels of neurotransmitters in the brain, including norepinephrine and dopamine (Cleveland Clinic, 2022). These neurotransmitters play a vital role in doing things like managing hyperactivity and impulses, improving the attention span, and eliminating executive dysfunction. It is important to remember that there are many ADHD medications, and not everyone responds the same to all of them.

THE HISTORY OF ADHD MEDICATION

It is important to know the history of a thing to truly understand it. ADHD and medical treatments for it have a rich, centuries old history that contributes to the way we perceive and treat ADHD even today.

The history of ADHD and medication options goes back probably farther than you realize. It all started in 1798, when a Scottish doctor named Sir Alexander Crichton discovered that some people were prone to hyperactivity and easily distracted, especially beginning earlier in life. In 1902, the first lectures on ADHD were held that ring true to today regarding women being less often diagnosed–but not less likely to have ADHD–than men. Approximately 30 years later came the discovery of something called 'hyperkinetic disease'. This "disease" affected children who were seemingly unable to sit still, as they were afflicted with hyper kinetic energy. Just five years later, the first ADHD medications began to be developed. The medication known as 'Ritalin' today was initially created in 1944– how fascinating!

But the history does not stop there. For several more decades, changes were made to how we think about, diagnose, and treat ADHD. One of the most notable changes is when ADHD got its new name. Originally, ADHD was referred to as ADD. It wasn't in the Diagnostic and Statistical Manual (DSM) until 1968, and it was renamed to ADD with and without hyperactivity in 1980. Seven years later, the American Psychological Association shifted the name to ADHD. In the most recent version of the DSM, the DSM-V or DSM-5, ADHD was officially classified with the three presentations of the disorder that I mentioned earlier. That's quite a history for one concept!

Understanding this history is a good thing, because it lets you know that quite literally centuries of work went into the diagnostic and medical aspects of treating ADHD. This should contribute some level of comfort to the fact that we do know that ADHD medications are safe; they'd not be on the market today if they were unsafe! People have lived out entire healthy lives after ADHD medication without any complications. It is an incredible feat only accomplished by being willing to take the risk.

COMMON ADHD MEDICATIONS

Adderall is the ADHD medication that, by name, most people are familiar with. You might be surprised to find out that there are dozens of medications for ADHD that you can try, but first, let's talk about Adderall; the one everyone's heard about.

Adderall is a medication that contains a mixture of amphetamine and dextroamphetamine (Drugs.com, 2017). These are both chemicals that stimulate the central nervous system, making this drug the best option for those who struggle with hyperactivity and impulse control. In other words, the stimulating components of this medication allow those who take it to be able to stay focused, pay attention, and exhibit more behavioral control. Some people also experienced improvements in organization and listening as well. Besides ADHD, Adderall has also been used to treat narcolepsy. If that sounds familiar, it is because this is exactly what the lady from the beginning was taking Adderall for! It just so happened that she had ADHD as well, and this medication did worlds of good for her, but that is enough about Adderall for now. It is the topic of the whole book; let's give these other medications a chance to shine!

Concerta

Another ADHD medication that you might have heard of goes by the name 'Concerta'. Concerta also stimulates the central nervous system, just like Adderall (drugs.com, 2019). It can also be taken to quell hyperactivity and impulse control. It comes in something called 'extended-release tablets', which release throughout the period of 24 hours instead of all at once like other medications. Usually, it is recommended that Concerta be taken with therapeutic help to provide the fullest effect.

It is considered a Schedule 2 controlled substance. What that means is that it is controlled and cannot be taken without strict adherence to medical advice. This is because many people abuse their medication, meaning that they take it in some manner other than how it is prescribed. This can lead to addiction, but keep in mind that taking your medication as prescribed is unlikely to have the same result. This is because a medical professional will slowly lower your dosage until you are off the medication in a safe and monitored way.

Speaking of the proper ways to take medication, there are some things to keep in mind. Concerta has a few key side effects to keep in mind before you start taking the medication, because some side effects can worsen or last. This is not something of major concern, however, as in most cases symptoms are temporary or non-existent. You should be mindful of these side effects just in case and inform your doctor if symptoms persist. These symptoms can include things like weight change, dizziness, nausea, trouble sleeping, headache, and similar side effects. If you have symptoms involving circulation changes, sudden wounds appearing, etc., it is recommended that you contact your doctor immediately.

There are also a few groups of people who should not take Concerta, which is the case with any stimulant medication. Because this medication can impact your blood pressure and heart rate, those with heart problems or hypertension should talk in depth with their doctor before taking this medication. You should also disclose to your doctor if you have a current mental illness, history of mental illnesses, or a family history of such as well, because this medication can interact negatively with those conditions if assurances are not made. Furthermore, people who are taking monoamine oxidase inhibitors (MAOIs) should avoid this medication due to some potentially deadly interactions. Finally, do not consume dexmethylphenidate alongside this medication; due to this chemical being similar to the ones already in Concerta, it can be dangerous to do so.

It might sound scary hearing all of those warnings, but rest assured that Concerta is a safe medication and understanding potential complications is what keeps you safe. Danger only arises when medications are used improperly, so be sure to disclose your complete medical history to your doctor.

Ritalin

In addition to Adderall and Concerta, a drug called 'Ritalin' may be used to treat ADHD, which is a medication you have likely heard of before. The primary chemical in Ritalin that makes it work is methylphenidate, which is another stimulant medication (Ritalin Oral: Uses, Side Effects, Interactions, Pictures, Warnings & Dosing - WebMD, n.d.). Much like Concerta, Ritalin uses this chemical to alter chemicals within the brain in order to elevate your ability to pay attention, focus on a specific activity at hand, control behavioral issues, and more.

Ritalin should be taken exactly as prescribed by your doctor. You should ideally take this medication about a half an hour prior to eating, but those with sensitive or upset stomachs might benefit from taking it with food. It is also important to keep in mind that taking Ritalin late in the day has the potential to keep you up. In addition, taking Ritalin at the same time every single day and in the same amounts is going to be best because this keeps the level of the drug consistent in your system. The dose your doctor gives you might seem low at first, but this is a safety precaution that accompanies the prescription of many forms of medication. This ensures that side effects are non-existent or tolerable, and it makes sure that you do not become addicted to a medication by using it irresponsibly. Your doctor may slowly raise or lower the levels of your Ritalin dose as needed.

All medications have side effects, unfortunately, and we must talk about the side effects of Ritalin in order to keep you safe. Most of the side effects are incredibly similar to those of Concerta, which is because these medications are all of the same type–stimulants. Side effects like nervousness, insomnia, eating issues, weight loss or gain, nausea, and headache might accompany the use of Ritalin, for example. It is important to let your doctor know if these side effects persist. In rare cases, signs of fainting or seizures may occur. Be sure to let your doctor know if you have symptoms of this or erectile dysfunction. Also, keep in mind that if your doctor has prescribed you this medication, it is because they've determined that the potential negatives outweigh how wonderful that this medication can be for you. Major side effects only occur in the most rare of cases, so do not worry too much about them.

It is also advised to let your doctor know about any pre-existing health conditions you may have that impact the heart, blood pressure, or your mental health before you begin this medication. These precautions sound similar to Concerta's precautions, which is for a reason. Likewise, avoid Ritalin if you take MOAIs as well, because the interaction can cause potentially deadly results. One major thing to keep in mind with Ritalin is that Ritalin can alter the results of brain scans or diagnostic testing for Parkinson's disease. As such, make sure to let a medical professional know if you are on Ritalin and plan to receive these tests.

Overall, Ritalin is one of the oldest and safest medications that can be offered for ADHD. It works for a lot of people, but do not worry–if Ritalin does not or did not work for you, there are plenty of other options to try.

Vyvanse

As I mentioned, there are other options outside of the ones that I have mentioned so far for ADHD medication. One such option includes Vyvanse. Vyvanse also goes by the name 'lisdexamfetamine', and it is used for ADHD treatment among other things (Drugs & Medications, 2019). It is recommended that Vyvanse be used in accordance with other treatment options like therapy, other medications, counseling, etc. Most medications in general are this way, meaning you will experience more strong and beneficial impacts by taking your medication in combination with therapy and other treatment methods. Vyvanse is another stimulant medication that helps balance or boost neurotransmitters in the brain. As far as other treatment options go, Vyvanse is also used for the treatment of binge eating disorder.

Vyvanse should be taken exactly as your doctor recommends, which will likely be once in the morning each day. Your doctor should let you know if you need to take this medication with or without food. Taking medications like Vyvanse in the afternoon or evening can cause insomnia due to the stimulating quality of the medication. Vyvanse comes in a few options. One option is a chewable tablet, which you should chew up thoroughly and then swallow. However, if you have been prescribed the capsule form, either swallow the capsule whole or mix the contents of it into a juice or food item; just make sure that it is something that is not hot. It is important that you do not do this in advance and prepare your doses as needed, otherwise the medication may not be as effective. As with the other options, be sure to take your Vyvanse at the same time each day. This helps the medication work better and prevents you from forgetting to take it.

There are some side effects that you should be aware of as well, which are a little different from the previous side effects I have mentioned. As such, it is important to keep in mind these little idiosyncratic differences for your safety. Some minor side effects you might experience when you first start taking Vyvanse include nausea or vomiting, loss of appetite, weight change, constipation, headache, irritability, and restlessness. If these side effects last or get worse, then it is important to let your doctor know. You should also monitor your blood pressure on this medication, as it can cause an increase in your blood pressure. Serious side effects that occur in rare cases include heart palpitations, blurry vision, hallucinations, suicidal thoughts, muscle twitching, and similar. If you experience these side effects or fainting, breathing issues, seizures, and weakness, get medical help immediately.

In addition, the previous health precautions regarding MAOIs and medical history apply to this medication as well; however, something specific you should pay attention to is how this medication may affect you. Vyvanse can cause dizziness, which means you should avoid driving or doing anything requiring alert mental states until this drug has settled in your system. It is also best to avoid alcohol or marijuana while taking this medication, as either substance can increase dizziness or the potential for overdose. You should also let your dentist know that you take this medication before dental surgery. Be sure to let your doctor know of any other medications you take as well.

Focalin XR

Another medication that your doctor might offer you for ADHD is Focalin XR. Focalin XR is another extended-release medication, which means that it slowly releases into your system throughout a 24-hour period. Focalin XR is used primarily to treat ADHD, and the main chemical component in it that allows for this medication to improve neurotransmitter levels is dexmethylphenidate (Focalin Oral: Uses, Side Effects, Interactions, Pictures, Warnings & Dosing - WebMD, n.d.). This stimulant medication allows for those who take it to pay better attention, focus, and control behavioral problems associated with ADHD. Usually, Focalin is prescribed once or twice a day, either with or without food, and the doses are both taken earlier in the day. However, your dose will be specially monitored by your doctor for individualized treatment.

You're probably familiar with the common side effects associated with ADHD medications by now, but I find it helpful and important to restate them each time due to the fact that these side effects are necessary to keep an eye on. For instance, taking Focalin may leave you with nausea, stomach cramps, appetite loss, dizziness, or feelings of jitters. Remember that it is important to advise your doctor if these side effects get worse or persist. Fainting, seizure, and heart attack like symptoms are rare, but potential side effects, indicating that you should seek medical attention immediately. Do not drive when you first start taking Focalin XR, and avoid excess substance use as well. Focalin should not be taken along with MAOIs either.

Strattera

The final main ADHD medication that we will talk about is Strattera. Strattera is also referred to as atomoxetine', and is used primarily for ADHD and its treatment (Drugs & Medications, 2019). Though, it is recommended that this medication be used in combination with other treatment options. It allows you to focus, avoid fidgeting, and concentrate far better. Strattera does this by balancing the neurotransmitters in your brain. This medication is usually prescribed to be taken 1-2 times a day. Unlike other medications, you cannot break open, crush, or chew this medication; it must be taken as is. All of the typical side effects apply to this medication, but with Strattera there is an increased risk of sexual side effects like lowered libido.

NON-STIMULANTS AND ANTI-DEPRESSANTS

Other types of medication are utilized for ADHD as well besides just stimulants. This means that there are options for you if you can't or do not want to take stimulant medication. Stimulants, however, are the most common treatment for ADHD and are used for most severe cases of ADHD. For 70-80% of the people who have tried ADHD medication, stimulants have been notably effective (Bhargava, 2008). That said, where stimulants do not work, there are different options. Non-stimulant options are available and are known to improve focus and impulsiveness. For example, your doctor might start by prescribing you anti-depressants to treat your ADHD. Anti-depressants can be used to treat ADHD itself, or can be used to treat the symptoms of depression or anxiety that often accompany ADHD. Common anti-depressants for ADHD include Wellbutrin, MAOIs, and Effexor. If stimulants are not the medication for you, consider asking your doctor about what other options are available.

CHAPTER SUMMARY

- ADHD medication can and often does work if prescribed by a responsible doctor in the proper dose.

- ADHD has three presentations that describe whether someone falls on the more hyperactive side of the scale or the more inattentive side.
- ADHD can be caused by things like genetics and brain function, but not diet or vaccines.
- ADHD was first noticed in the late 1700s, and by 1945, we had our first medication for it.
- Adderall, Vyvanse, Concentra, Ritalin, Daytrana, and Focalin XR are the most common ADHD medications.
- Non-stimulants and anti-depressants can be used as an off-label treatment for ADHD too.

That's quite a lot of generalized and basic information about ADHD and potential treatment options. It should be noted that, of course, there are far more treatment options available. This chapter simply aimed to key you in on the major and main treatment options that are typically offered. You now understand what ADHD is, the basic history of its treatment, and the essentials surrounding six different ADHD medications. In the next chapter, together we will go into more depth regarding Adderall, including how it is taken and who it is right for.

2

A CLOSER LOOK AT ADDERALL

Knowledge is power. Information is liberating. Education is the premise of progress, in every society, in every family. –Kofi Annan

The success stories I have read have inspired me to take a closer look into Adderall, as well as develop a stronger, more assured level of trust in this medication. There are so many success stories that you can find online, where people who have taken Adderall have shared their experience. For example, Reddit is a hotspot for stories like this. In one story, user NotAnotherMillenial describes the way that prior to Adderall, they didn't have the confidence to go to college because of how low their grades were (ILikePotatoesNotYams, 2020). After becoming medicated, they realized that they are actually a very intelligent individual, but ADHD made it difficult to excel academically. Many other users share similar inspiring college success stories like these. Another user, TranseDeRever, describes how Adderall allowed them to turn their life around, recovering their mental health and allowing them to engage in hobbies and academia with life and passion both.

All of this goes to show that while it is possible to have a bad experience with medication, with proper monitoring by your doctor, your experience with Adderall and other ADHD medications could be phenomenal. It could change your life, but you do have to give it a chance to do so. If your doctor has prescribed you anything at all, it is because they have decided that any negative impacts of the medication are worth the advantages. And if you do have a less than enjoyable medication experience, I can tell you that it is not going to be like that with every single medication.

Adderall has changed the lives of many people, myself included. It is thoroughly worth learning about, so let's talk about how it is typically intended to be taken and the specific benefits that Adderall has to offer.

TAKING ADDERALL

Adderall comes in different dosage options, anywhere between tablets of 5mg and 30mg (Adderall for ADHD/ADD: Uses, Dosages, Side Effects, Treatment, 2022). It is usually prescribed to be taken once or twice a day, earlier in the day so as to avoid insomnia or other sleep-related side effects. Many people who are medicated for ADHD prefer this medication to other ADHD medications, like Ritalin, because as the medication wears off, it seems to have less side effects when taking Adderall as opposed to certain other medications. Furthermore, Adderall doses last longer than other medications, making it a wonderful option for people looking to take one dose and leave it at that.

Certain groups of people should, however, avoid taking Adderall. Adderall is safe for children three and older, but anyone who has even slightly high blood pressure should avoid taking this medication altogether. Additionally, people who are prone to mania, such as those with bipolar or borderline personality disorder, should consult their doctor before taking this medication. Finally, those with a history of drug abuse should exercise extreme caution when taking Adderall, as if taken improperly, this medication can become habit forming.

From a medical perspective, it is thought that ADHD is a result of imbalanced neurotransmitters (Kennedy, 2020). Neurotransmitters are responsible for passing messages back and forth in the brain–among other things–and experts have noticed a correlation between lower levels of the neurotransmitters dopamine and norepinephrine and those who have ADHD. Adderall works because it causes your brain to release more of these neurotransmitters, allowing for easier focus, impulse control, and more. It also impacts the body in a variety of ways. Some of these ways allow for the medication to work better, while others explain the potential side effects that could arise. Understanding how this medication could impact your body will allow you to make a more sound decision with your doctor.

For example, Adderall has certain impacts on the central nervous system (Hobbs, 2014). The positive effects that this medication can provide as a result of its effect on the central nervous system include making you feel more alert, increasing your ability to focus, and imbuing you with a sense of calm. However, some of the negative side effects might include nervousness or restlessness. It all depends on how the medication impacts you specifically. Beyond that, one serious way that Adderall affects the body involves the circulatory and respiratory systems. For example, I have mentioned that Adderall can raise your blood pressure.

This is because it can cause blood vessels to contract and speed up your heart rate, impacting blood circulation in some cases. This is why those with high blood pressure or heart conditions might benefit from avoiding stimulant medication.

You might experience some impacts to your digestive system as well. The chemicals found within Adderall can raise the levels of glucose in your digestive system, leading to things like stomach pain, nausea, or constipation. You might also experience appetite loss or weight fluctuations, especially weight loss, while taking Adderall. These side effects usually subside a week or two after beginning this medication. If you experience issues with an upset stomach or eating when you first start taking Adderall, it may be that you need to eat with your medication. A final way that Adderall might impact your body pertains to your skin. In the rare case that you are allergic to Adderall or the chemicals in it, you might experience hives or a rash. If you do, stop taking this medication and immediately let your doctor know.

Another important part of the body–because it controls the whole body–is the brain, and Adderall clearly has unique impacts upon the brain and how it works. Adderall impacts the brain by increasing neurotransmitters, as I have mentioned before. It is important to know, however, that taking Adderall only "works" for people who actually have ADHD (What Does Adderall Do to Your Brain? It Depends | Caron, n.d.). For someone without ADHD, it can seem as though Adderall makes you feel more wakeful, able to cope with stress, etc., but in the long-run, this is an incredibly dangerous drug to misuse. For people who DO have ADHD, taking Adderall simply elevates neurotransmitter levels back to their "normal" amount. We will talk about some of the benefits of this shift in the next section.

I understand that it might sound confusing–why do I keep recommending you something with side effects, going back and forth between the positives and the negatives? Well, it is because I believe in informed consent to medical treatment. You should be aware of the potential risks of anything you put into your body, but that does not mean that those risks will occur. It is very rare for a medication like Adderall to negatively impact someone severely. To ease your mind, I want to spend a bit of time talking exclusively about the benefits of Adderall.

BENEFITS OF ADDERALL

Adderall, as we've seen from success stories, has the power to change one's life. It can be the difference between night and day for someone–transforming a D student into a 4.0 student in just days. It can make you feel so much better and have so many positive impacts on your overall life. Adderall is beneficial because it eases the main symptoms of ADHD that prevent those with the disorder from functioning within society in a way that is perceived to be "normal". You might struggle with focus and impulse control, for example, which is something that medications like Adderall can alleviate. In fact, for 70% of adults and up to 80% of children, Adderall was noted to be incredibly effective (Bhandari, 2021). Symptoms that typically improve when someone starts Adderall include fidgeting, hyper-activity, conversational interruptions, and more.

The main benefits of Adderall enjoyed by people who take it surround being able to pay better attention, focus on an activity at hand, and control behavioral issues. We've talked about how Adderall does this—it improves the levels of neurotransmitters in the brain— but what is in Adderall that allows it to do this? Adderall combines the substances amphetamine and dextroamphetamine. These two chemical compounds serve as stimulants to the central nervous system. In other words, they provide a sense of alertness to your body. For those with ADHD, it can often feel like you have enough energy already, but the stimulating boost of these substances is actually incredible for focus.

These chemicals are responsible for boosting your levels of dopamine and norepinephrine.

As I have mentioned, one of the main benefits of Adderall is that it improves both concentration and focus. This can benefit you in both career and academic environments. You might not even know how ADHD is negatively impacting you at school or work. So, allow me to provide you with some examples.

ADHD can cause it to be difficult to focus at work, especially if you are not particularly interested in the activities at hand. If you, for example, work a desk job where you have to file a lot of paperwork, ADHD can mean that you take way longer than others do to complete the same tasks. You might become distracted easily, focusing on anything but what you need to be doing, or you may find yourself having difficulties starting, finishing, or keeping up with what you need to be doing at work. This is one common way that ADHD impacts your career–lowered performance means you can get in trouble with your boss and lose your job, promotions, status, etc.

Similar impacts can happen at school. This is the most common way children are affected–with teachers and parents commonly commenting on the ways their children behave in school–but it can impact adults in college as well. You might find that you excel in one area of college but completely underperform in another, even if those areas fall within the same subject or course. This often causes students to feel stupid or incompetent, even when that is not the case.

Imagine the difference ADHD medication would make if this is what you face. It can completely alleviate all of the symptoms you are feeling, changing a dark or gloomy life littered with a lack of productivity and focus into one where you can achieve anything you want to do with ease. ADHD medication makes it easier to function in so many settings, which is why people describe such stellar effects.

Another set of benefits stemming from ADHD medication is the ability to listen better and organize tasks more effectively. Let's start with the listening aspect. A lot of people who have ADHD struggle to listen to what others are saying because focusing for an extended amount of time on one particular task can be rather challenging. This is especially the case when listening to someone's voice. With ADHD medication, you gain the ability to focus on what others are saying. Furthermore, it becomes easier to avoid interruptions in conversation because you can more easily pay attention to the flow of the conversation. This improves relationships and your overall ability to communicate by allowing conversations to be more smooth.

With regard to the ability to organize tasks more effectively, let me introduce you to a scenario. Imagine you work from home. Let's say you have a home office where you do the vast majority of your work, and it has a desk, computer, bookshelves, and some random stuff from around the house in it—a sewing project here, an art project there. Imagine this place in your mind, and then imagine what you would end up doing if you had to work in this environment. Chances are you wouldn't be able to get any work done; instead, you would sit down to work, decide to finish that sewing project, dust the bookshelf, go online shopping for a new chair, watch a movie, etc., until suddenly the deadline has arrived and nothing has been done.

If you know what I mean with that scenario, you are definitely not alone. This is the reality that a lot of people with ADHD face, but it is also the reality that completely evaporates for many people with ADHD once they start medications like Adderall. Someone who lives with a life like the following scenario can benefit highly from becoming medicated, because ADHD medications like Adderall significantly improve our overall ability to organize tasks. This means that you would be able to sit down and get your work done, making activities like office improvements, cleaning, and personal projects something distinctly different.

You would then be able to grant individual time for each task.

Imagine this, now. You still work from home, in the same office that looks the same way. Thanks to your new medication, you are much more in tune with what you feel and why, because you are not so overwhelmed constantly. You enter the office and it bothers you because there's so much going on–things that do not belong in your office galore! You notice it is a tad bit distracting, but you really have to get some work done. So, you sit down to work, getting all of your tasks done without a problem. No stress at all, wow! Then, you go to tackle the clutter in your office, hitting one area at a time before moving on to the next. In the time it would take you to, halfway, do 10 tasks, you have completely finished those same 10 and feel no stress associated with doing so at all! That's the power Adderall and other medications can have over your life; they can make you feel like a wholly new person in the best of ways.

An additional benefit of Adderall is that it can be used to treat certain sleep disorders, most specifically narcolepsy. Narcolepsy is a sleep disorder where you struggle to stay awake during the day. It is more than just excessive sleepiness–narcolepsy causes unexpected passing out or blacking out, even in situations where it is inappropriate to do so. It is a sleep disorder that impacts many people, and in response and for treatment, ADHD medications may be prescribed. The stimulating impact that these medications can have is incredibly helpful in allowing those with narcolepsy to stay awake despite their disorder. Creating more alertness for the central nervous system, medications like Adderall can help keep you awake during the daytime, tiring yourself out before nighttime. This can take someone who is used to missing half their day from a life like that to a life where they experience things in full.

It is a life changing medication, but unfortunately, this reason is also the explanation for why many people abuse Adderall. For many college students and others who do not have ADHD, medications like Adderall can be tempting because they help create wakefulness. This is one reason why it is a medication that is often misused during school, exam times, etc., by people without ADHD or people who know someone willing to "share" their medication. Furthermore, ADHD medications like Adderall can create a sense of euphoria in people without ADHD who take it. This provides another tempting explanation for those without ADHD to begin taking Adderall and other medication recreationally.

Because of this, it is important that I tell you this— misusing medications, especially ones for ADHD is the BEST way to cause a negative experience with medication. Sharing your medication, taking medication that is not prescribed to you, or misusing medication that is prescribed to you can lead to addiction, negative side effects, and even death if the wrong person gets their hands on stimulating medication. Because of this, it is incredibly important to keep your medication to yourself, and to encourage anyone who is interested in Adderall or similar medications to take their questions to a doctor. It is for their safety and yours, physically, mentally, and legally.

The benefits of ADHD medication being used as prescribed do not stop there. As I mentioned earlier, ADHD medications can help you excel academically. Your focus will improve drastically, and because of the ability to engage with the world in ways mentioned before, academic performance can skyrocket.

Similarly, ADHD medications can allow you to notice improvements in your relationships. A lot of tensions exist between partners in a relationship where only one person has something like ADHD. However, when the partner with ADHD becomes medicated, a whole new world can open up for that relationship. The partner who has ADHD and is medicated will be more able to listen to and remember what the other person is saying (Pera, 2022). Adderall improves the ability to focus and improves memory too, which means that you will be able to listen to your partner in a more effective way and remember important things like dates, agreements, and promises as well. This can resolve so many tensions in a relationship where the partner without ADHD feels resentment or sadness at the fact that their partner–you–struggles to listen and remember things. It is neither of your faults, but ADHD medication can resolve the issue for both of you.

Another benefit that those in relationships experience is improved safety. A lot of times, people with ADHD have issues with impulse control and other behavioral issues. This can affect life in two main, yet dangerous, areas, depending on the individual–finances and driving. Financially, those with unmedicated ADHD struggle with budgeting and wise spending habits. It can be incredibly easy to walk into a store and spend all sorts of money on things that are not needed, even if it harms your overall way of life as a partnership. In fact, spending like this can become a compulsion, making it more difficult for the partnership to thrive, both as together and as the individuals who make that partnership up. In addition, those with unmedicated may be especially prone to making rash or impulsive decisions that make their driving habits unsafe. This can make it feel incredibly unsafe to go out with a partner because they will be prone to excessive spending and unsafe driving. However, once someone becomes medicated, it can be much easier to avoid these impulses. A tricky driver or impulse spender can transform into someone who is careful with their money and driving, respectively. This can save a relationship easily.

Additionally, those who become medicated for their ADHD are more capable of handling situations with empathy and kindness. When you have ADHD, it can be really difficult to listen to the thoughts of others because you are so distracted by your own, but when your ADHD is under control, it is more likely that you are able to find a succinct and flawless balance between your needs and the needs of your partner. This would allow your partner to feel secure and cared for within the relationship. There are several other relationship benefits that you might experience with your partner once you become medicated as well. This includes being more reliable and far more enjoyable to be around once you are no longer plagued by the things that you worry about as a result of your ADHD. Overall, you will be a much happier person.

As you can see, there are so many benefits to getting medicated for ADHD. Adderall can benefit you in almost every aspect of your life if taken properly, so it is well worth considering if you have ADHD.

CHAPTER SUMMARY

- ADHD medication has been widely successful for many people, and many of their success stories are available online.
- Adderall comes in different dosage tablets, from 5-30mg.
- It can be taken 1-2 times a day.
- Do not take Adderall if you are on MAOIs or have issues with your heart or blood pressure.
- Adderall is often preferable to Ritalin because it lasts longer and has less side effects as it wears off.
- Those with drug abuse issues should avoid Adderall.
- ADHD results from imbalanced neurotransmitters, specifically dopamine and norepinephrine, which are balanced by Adderall.
- Adderall can impact the central nervous system, skin, lungs, blood pressure, and more.
- You might experience weight fluctuations while taking Adderall.

- Hives or a rash indicate a potential allergic reaction.
- You should stop taking your medication immediately if this occurs.
- Adderall impacts the brain by balancing neurotransmitters, but people without ADHD should never take Adderall due to addiction issues.
- Adderall is effective for 70-80% of people who take it.
- ADHD medication will help you improve your ability to focus, organize, concentrate, etc.
- Adderall is also used to treat certain sleep disorders because of its status as a stimulant medication.
- Adderall can improve relationships and academic performance.

The ADHD success stories alone are enough to inspire me. I think ADHD medication is well worth the risk if you need it. There are many options for medication that can suit your needs and desires, and while some negative side effects may accompany your medication, 70-80% of the people who take it experience benefits. That's a high number and well worth considering medication as a result of. Furthermore, you are likely to experience benefits, both mental and physical, from taking medication for your ADHD. You deserve to have your own success story just like we talked about in the beginning of this chapter. My hope is that the benefits presented in this chapter inspire you to seek your own ADHD medication prescription if you think it is right for you. Now, you understand the various side effects and benefits that accompany Adderall, which apply to similar ADHD medications as well. In the next chapter, we will talk about how to pursue an ADHD medication prescription and what to do with your medication once it has been prescribed.

3

TAKING ADDERALL AND GETTING APPROVED

Bravery is when you walk into a battle you are not sure of winning. —Jeffrey Fry

As you may already know, you can't get Adderall without a prescription. There's a good reason for such, but let's talk about the primary reason that people without a prescription might seek out Adderall. Studies have shown that college students are more likely to "try" Adderall that is not prescribed to them than others their age who are not in college (Where Families Find Answers on Substance Use | Partnership for Drug-Free Kids, 2017). In fact, 5-35% of college students have taken Adderall that is not prescribed to them. The easy access to Adderall is part of what provokes people to take Adderall that is not prescribed to them.

Why do I tell you this? Well, it may seem crass, but I think these statistics just indicate how positive of a medication it can be. People seek it out for the myriad benefits it can offer, even if they should not. Additionally, understanding that this situation puts people at risk allows you to comprehend the reason why the process behind getting a prescription from a reliable doctor is so important. This chapter will focus on everything you need to know about getting a prescription, taking it properly, what dosages can be expected, and how the medication impacts both children and adults.

WHY IS A PRESCRIPTION NEEDED?

Most medications need a prescription. The ones that do not are called "over the counter" medications, because you can get them from the customer's side of a pharmacy counter. These medications can be effective, but they will not do it all—most OTC medications you will find are for things like minor pain and allergies. Something like Adderall will never be prescribed over the counter due to the ways in which it can be misused, which means that you have to get a prescription for it.

From a more technical perspective, ADHD medications require a prescription because they're referred to as 'controlled substances' (Liao, n.d.). Controlled substances are regulated by something called 'schedules' based on how safe they are and the potentiality that they will be misused. Most ADHD medications fall into Schedule II, because they have quite the possibility to be misused but are not the most misused medication out there either. Because of the potential to misuse and the dangerous side effects that can arise from taking more of your medication than you are prescribed, it is important to take it as directed. This both limits danger and dependency, keeping you as safe as possible.

HOW TO GET A PRESCRIPTION

Getting a prescription for a new medication can be daunting, especially for a medication like Adderall, which requires a new prescription every single month you take it. It can feel like you have done something "wrong" by approaching your doctor with a specific medication in mind due to the stigma surrounding this. If you feel like you need Adderall or similar stimulant medications, there is a right way and a wrong way to go about obtaining that medication. The right way always involves going through a licensed medical practitioner.

So, how do you do that to get something like Adderall? First, it is important to understand who can safely prescribe you medications like Adderall. Other people may tell you that they can "prescribe" or provide medications like Adderall to you, but for your safety and theirs, it is always best to go to one of the following medical professionals. Physicians–including your primary care physician and neurologist–are among the first group able to safely prescribe Adderall (Reale, 2022). It is best that if you plan to talk to your physician about this kind of treatment, you let them know ahead of time, as a longer appointment may be necessary to discuss options. Clinical psychologists can prescribe ADHD medication to you safely as well because they have been specially trained to do so. Furthermore, you can seek out a psychiatrist for a prescription, but most psychiatrists do not offer therapeutic services, which makes the use of medication more effective overall.

Once you have decided who you will go to for your prescription, you can begin the process of actually getting prescribed the medication. The first thing that you will need to do is book an appointment with your preferred medical professional. Make a list of the symptoms that are bothering you or that you think lend to you needing an ADHD medication, and write down when each symptom began. Let your doctor know about any conditions or health problems you may have, as well as any medications you take, and you are all set on your end. The doctor will probably conduct various tests in order to gain further insight into what's going on, and then provide you with a prescription to the medication that they think will be most effective for you.

In addition to medication, you might want to pursue some other options that will increase the likelihood that your medication will work. For example, therapy that accompanies medication often makes it more effective. You might also try exercising and sleeping enough, developing daily routines, seeking accommodations for work and/or school, and more. Remember that Adderall has to be prescribed monthly, so you will likely need to visit with your doctor each month in order to continue this treatment option.

There are two more important things to keep in mind regarding these medications, which include OTC medications and travel. I cannot express enough that there are no approved ADHD medications that you will be able to find over the counter, and anyone who claims otherwise is being dishonest with you. Furthermore, something to keep in mind when you take any medication is travel considerations. If you plan to travel when you will need a refill before you return, be sure to talk to your doctor about the options available to you before you go. This way, you do not find yourself stranded somewhere without your medication.

METHODS FOR APPROVAL

As I mentioned, you can obtain ADHD medication in person through discussing your options with a licensed medical practitioner who has the ability to either prescribe you medication or refer you to someone who can. This is often the easiest and simplest way to get these kinds of medications, while also keeping you safe in the meantime. Two other options that people ask me about regarding medication for ADHD are online prescription of the medication and self-prescription. Out of these three options, I would absolutely recommend seeking a prescription from an in-person doctor first and foremost. However, let me talk to you about these other options that are available.

First, we will address online prescriptions. Through something called 'telehealth services', which are essentially virtual medical appointments, many doctors can prescribe certain kinds of medication and have them mailed directly to you. This is a particularly effective and valuable method for those with disabilities or those who do not have the funds to seek a traditional doctor; however, there are certain medications that cannot typically be prescribed via a telehealth doctor due to safety concerns.

You can absolutely seek an Adderall prescription online, as many doctors do prescribe Adderall and other ADHD medications through telehealth and telemedicine, but one important thing to consider is the cost. Because of the circumstances surrounding telemedicine, some virtual doctors charge several hundreds of dollars for the initial meeting and more for further meetings and the prescription, and this does not include the cost of the medication itself. This means that, unfortunately for many, it is far more cost-effective to seek a prescription from a doctor you can meet with in person. Furthermore, telemedicine often gets a bad rapport for being notoriously unreliable at providing consistent and sound treatment options. This is something you should consider thoroughly before conducting a telehealth appointment for the purpose of obtaining ADHD medication.

If you are completely set on taking this route, there are steps you must take in order to be able to do this successfully. First, you need to select a provider and schedule an appointment. In order to weed out which practitioners you can go to, first consider those in your state (How to Get Prescribed Adderall for ADHD Online | Klarity, 2022). Because Adderall is a controlled substance, providers can only prescribe it to those inside of the same state. Once you have found a provider that looks like a good fit, see if they specialize in ADHD. If not, it is likely that they will not prescribe medication for ADHD either.

Then, you have to book and attend the appointment before a prescription can get to you. During a telehealth diagnostic appointment, your doctor will try to see if Adderall is the right medication for the goals you are trying to meet, and may formally diagnose you with ADHD if you haven't been already. Once all of that is done, your prescription will either be delivered to you or your local pharmacy. You will have follow up appointments with your doctor where they continue to prescribe medication to you and monitor how the medication impacts your condition.

There are also a few things that you might want to be prepared to discuss at your telehealth appointment for ADHD. Your doctor is going to ask you a lot of questions, and it is important that you answer them accurately despite what answer you think that they "want" to hear. This ensures that you get the best and most appropriate treatment available for you specifically. Moreover, you should be prepared to provide a full medical history to your doctor so that they can understand your background and prescribe the best medication for your needs.

Overall, it is possible to seek an online prescription for Adderall or other ADHD medications if this seems like the right option for you. Understanding your options and seeking out help according to the steps above is the best way to get the help that you need in a timely manner.

Another option many people consider or wonder about is self-prescription. Self-prescription refers to the act of a medical provider prescribing medication to themselves or family members (Mcilvena, 2022). This can seem like a very tempting option to get medications like Adderall or other stimulants, but there are several things to keep in mind regarding self-prescription. Regarding non-controlled substances, you will need to look up the individual laws where you live to understand how the law views self-prescription; however, it is important to understand that self-prescription of controlled substances is illegal in practically every case. This is not just to make your life more difficult. Self-prescription is illegal because of ethical concerns, where you might prescribe something impulsively that is not actually in the best interest of a patient, yourself included. Self-prescribing medication might be warranted in an emergency, but otherwise, you should avoid it altogether unless you are willing to lose your medical license.

Without a doubt, the best options for someone seeking medication for ADHD, be it Adderall or another medication, include seeking in person treatment and telemedicine, in that order. These are the only approved avenues through which you can seek treatment of this variety, as other options are illegal due to the potential to put you into harm's way. If you are interested in medication for your ADHD, get help from a medical professional–other than yourself–who is licensed to do so.

TAKING YOUR MEDICATIONS

So, you have been prescribed Adderall. What now? Well, you have to take it, of course, but there are a lot of things to consider when it comes to taking medication, especially if this is your first time doing so. When you first get prescribed a medication, your doctor will provide you with a medication guide that often accompanies your prescription each time it is filled (Drugs & Medications, 2019). You should read through this each time you get a refill on your medication in order to refresh your memory about how to take your medication. Generally speaking, Adderall is taken orally with or without food, depending on what your doctor has asked you to do. However, if you feel like you get sick from taking this medication on an empty stomach, eat before or with your medication to eliminate that side effect. Most often, patients are prescribed Adderall one to three times a day, starting when they first wake up in the morning.

As you continue taking your medication, your doctor may adjust your dose in order to find which dose is right for you. Sometimes, this means raising or lowering the amount of medication that you take in order to see the most benefit from it. Regardless, it is important to take your medication at the same time each day in order to see the most benefits; most medications build up in the system in order to work best. It is also important that you do not abruptly stop taking this medication without medical advice, as doing so may result in withdrawal symptoms. These include sleeping issues, mood changes, or physical illness. In order to prevent this, if your doctor deems it worthwhile to take you off of your medication, your doctor will do something called 'tapering'. During tapering, your dose is slowly lowered until you have been completely weaned off of the medication in order to prevent symptoms of withdrawal.

Again, it is incredibly important that you take your medication exactly how it is prescribed, otherwise it is not going to work the way that it is meant to. If you have concerns or questions about your treatment, consult your doctor or a medical professional before making any changes.

DOSAGES

With any medication, different dosages are prescribed to different people based on varying factors, including age, severity of symptoms, etc. In order to prevent complications and to ensure that the medication prescribed is right for you, your doctor will often prescribe you a low dose to start out, and then increase the dosage as needed. For adults, the dosage typically begins at 5mg one to two times a day or as needed until your doctor is satisfied with the progress of treatment. However, the dosage is a little different for the extended-release version of Adderall, which is often prescribed to people who are forgetful, new to medication, or would otherwise benefit from the consistent release it offers. Adults usually begin with a 20mg extended-release capsule that releases Adderall into the system slowly over the course of a 24-hour period, keeping the levels of Adderall in your body consistent and allowing for better effects.

If you are learning about Adderall for a child, a similar concept is applied to their dosages; they are prescribed a low dose and then slowly moved up as needed. However, with children, that dosage typically begins at 2.5mg a day instead of the 5 mg once or twice a day typically prescribed to adults. This is because their bodies are smaller and need to metabolize less of a drug to see the benefits. Your child might be prescribed extended-release medication if they are young or go to school in order to prevent forgetfulness or distractions that medication can often cause. This will usually come in the form of a 10mg dosage which only has to be taken once a day. Extended-release medications are often preferable due to this fact–you only have to take them once a day to experience the same benefits.

After you or your child has been taking Adderall for between two and six weeks, your doctor might raise the amount of medication you are taking. This happens because the initial level of medication has settled in your system, meaning that your doctor can tell now if you would benefit from an elevated dosage of the medication. For children, the dose of Adderall usually caps off at 40mg, meaning that only in rare cases will a doctor prescribe more than 40mg to a child.

As mentioned previously, Adderall and other ADHD medications can be used to treat the symptoms of sleep disorders like narcolepsy. Interestingly enough, these cases are treated the same adults with the condition begin with a 5mg capsule and slowly move up to higher dosages, but they rarely exceed 60mg.

Understanding how these dosages work is important to understanding the progression of your treatment. If you have any questions about the dosage of your medication, be sure to ask your doctor or pharmacist about it.

ISSUES WITH REFILLS

Every day, many people experience issues with getting their medication refilled. This should not dissuade you from taking medication, however. Instead, understanding how to combat and resolve some of these common problems is in your best interest. Before we get started, remember that it is likely not your pharmacist's fault that they can't fill your prescription. In fact, your pharmacist would love to fill your medication, but in a lot of cases, their hands are tied and they, or the company they work for, could get into major trouble for making an exception and filling it anyway. Instead of getting mad at the pharmacist, let's learn about the common issues with refills that people experience, as well as how to overcome them.

Briefly, let's go over whether or not a pharmacist has the right to refuse to fill a prescription. Generally speaking, your pharmacist can refuse to fill a prescription for the following reasons (Why Your Pharmacist Can't Fill Your Prescription — and What to Do about It, n.d.):

- It is not considered to be a proper treatment for something. In other words, if a doctor tries to prescribe an antidepressant for pain management, the pharmacist will probably refuse to fill it.
- They know that it will cause you harm in some way.
- Your pharmacist can't verify that the prescription is legitimate.
- In rare cases, religious reasons allow for exemption from filling certain prescriptions (though a different pharmacist can fill it).

Unfortunately for some people, all of these reasons are valid and legal to deny someone a prescription. There are many more specific causes for a prescription to be unfillable as well.

For example, if the prescription is missing information, it can't be filled. In most states, your pharmacy needs to have your name and address, the name and dose of the medication, the form of medication prescribed, how many tablets or capsule are prescribed, directions, number of refills, promise date, your doctor's name or contact info, and their signature to confirm that the prescription is legitimate. For controlled substances like ADHD medication, additional information will need to be provided. Because pharmacies receive this information from your doctor directly, if any information is missing, they can contact your doctor. Problems like these are usually resolved within a day or two.

Another reason that your pharmacist may decline to fill your medication is that it is difficult to read. This is another case that will necessitate the pharmacy contacting your medical provider. On your end, update your contact information with the pharmacy if you notice that your prescription is difficult to read. This ensures that the pharmacy has a direct way to contact you in the case that they have trouble reading your prescription as well. Because they can usually have this resolved within a day, it should not be any cause for significant worry.

There's one really common situation that you likely will not encounter with ADHD medications, but should still be aware of in case it does happen. That's the case of a prescription being unable to be filled due to the fact that it has to be ordered. If you have never taken medication before, you might not know this, but most pharmacies do not have every medication in the world already on hand. Instead, pharmacies will order medications that are rarer, expensive, or low in stock to be delivered to the pharmacy before it can be filled. Occasionally this happens, and it can cause a few days of delay in getting your medication to you. Rest assured that the pharmacists understand your concern and are trying to get your medication to you as quickly as possible. Backorder and shortages may occur as well, and this is something that currently is impacting the ability of those with ADHD to get their medication. This is because more people need the medication faster than it can be produced, resulting in a shortage of medications like Adderall. This cannot be helped, and as a result your doctor may prescribe you something similar that is abundant right now in order to help you until the medication shortage subsides. This is the best and safest option available during a medication shortage.

Your pharmacist might reject your medication for another reason as well. If they notice that two medications you are being prescribed can have a dangerous or even deadly interaction, then for your safety they may decline to fill the prescription until your doctor speaks with them on the matter. If your doctor has prescribed you an ADHD medication that can have an interaction with something else you are taking, then one of two scenarios is true: Either they were unaware of other medications you are taking, which you should promptly notify them of, or they have deemed the benefits outweigh any potential interactions or risks that may arise from taking the medications in combination. However, your pharmacy cannot be sure that your doctor was aware of all other medications unless they contact them, which means you might have to wait a few hours to hear about a prescription refill.

Something else to keep in mind is technical errors. The pharmacists cannot control when their computers go down, and as preferable as it might be for them to just give you your medication and deal with the system when it is up, they can't do that. This is because Adderall and other ADHD medications are controlled substances. They cannot verify your identity without their system, and if someone other than you picks up the medication, not only will the pharmacy get in trouble, but you will not be able to have it filled again to pick it up yourself. This is a legal measure in place to prevent abuse of controlled substances. Similarly to how they can't control computer outages, pharmacists also can't control the things that your insurance company decides. If the insurance company declines to pay for your medication for whatever reason, you must contact them directly; the pharmacy can't do anything besides accept an out of pocket payment.

Beyond these reasons, there are some stimulant specific reasons medications might not get filled. It is common that a pharmacy will refuse to "refill" a stimulant medication because stimulant medications cannot typically have refills (Center, 2022). Typically, if your doctor tells you that they have sent in refills of your medication, what actually happened is that they sent several prescriptions for the same medication, but no refills. In other words, you might have three Adderall prescriptions but zero "refills". Because of how pharmacies operate, if you ask to have your Adderall refilled, they will likely tell you that no refills are available. Instead, ask whether or not you have any prescriptions on file that can be filled; you will likely have better luck that way.

It is also important to understand that prescriptions expire, typically after 90 days in the case of stimulant medications. Because of this, if you wait more than a certain amount of time to fill your prescription, you will not be able to fill it unless you call your doctor and they prescribe you the medication again. This is in place to prevent the abuse of stimulants.

It is also good to understand how the process of transferring medications works. If, for example, you want your prescription transferred to a pharmacy that is more convenient for you, with many stimulant medications you can't just facilitate that transition yourself. In other words, while some medications can be transferred from pharmacy to pharmacy without issues, controlled substances are often more complicated. If your pharmacy will not let you transfer the prescription on your own, you will have to call your doctor and have the medication prescribed at the new pharmacy. My recommendation is that you check with the new pharmacy that your medication is in stock before transferring, otherwise you risk a longer wait time. Ensure that the medication and correct dosage are in stock before you call your doctor or try to transfer your medication.

On a final note, your pharmacy can't refill or prescribe you more than 30 days of a stimulant medication at once for legal and safety reasons. As such, before you get your prescription refilled or call the pharmacy, check the date on your bottle. If, for instance, you picked that bottle up on the 15th of the month, you likely will not be able to pick the new medication up before the 14th or 15th of the following month.

CHAPTER SUMMARY

- ADHD medication has been wrongfully used by 5-35% of college-aged students.

- A prescription is necessary for medications, like Adderall, and for good reason too.
- Some reasons that you need a prescription for Adderall include that Adderall can be addictive or dangerous if taken improperly and that it is a Schedule II substance.
- The only people who can safely provide an Adderall prescription are physicians, clinical psychologists, and psychiatrists.
- Schedule an appointment with your doctor, bringing along a list of symptoms that are bothering you and when they started, in order to begin the process of seeking a diagnosis and/or medication.
- Remember that OTC options for ADHD have not been approved and that you will need to make special arrangements for your medication if you plan to travel for extended periods of time.
- Telehealth is an option, but not a very cost-effective or reliable one. It is often better to get a prescription in person.
- You can seek a telemedical prescription by finding a provider in your state and booking an appointment.
- Self-prescribing is illegal.

- Adderall is typically taken 1-3 times a day, starting first thing in the morning.
- Do not abruptly stop your medication.
- Children are started at 2.5mg once a day or 10mg extended release, whereas adults are started at 5mg one to two times a day or 20mg extended release.
- There are many reasons a prescription might not be fillable, but understanding how to avoid these issues will help you persevere.

Now that you understand the circumstances surrounding taking medications for ADHD and refilling them, it should be a lot easier and more comforting to begin the process of taking your medication or seeking out a prescription. Remember that your doctor will start you on a lower dose of many medications–Adderall included–before elevating the dose. Be sure to tell them of any side effects, health conditions, or other medications you take in order to avoid complications. Speaking of side effects, in the next chapter we will talk about every potential side effect that Adderall can have, allowing you to be prepared and knowledgeable on what you can potentially expect when you start taking this medication.

4

SIDE EFFECTS OF ADDERALL

Don't ever take a fence down until you know why it was put up. —Robert Frost

During the year of 2020, over five million people aged 12 and older abused prescription stimulants like the ADHD medication, Adderall (Geoffrion, 2023). Because of what Adderall is composed of—amphetamines—misusing the medication can cause tolerance or dependence. Those who misuse Adderall by taking Adderall that is not prescribed to them, or by using their prescribed Adderall incorrectly, are at risk of either of these things, as well as the potential to suffer from many of the other side effects that result from taking Adderall. The truth is that no medication is without side effects, but misusing a medication drastically increases the chances that you will face negative side effects and dependency without the medication even working in the first place.

I'm not saying these things, nor did I include this chapter, with the intention of scaring you. Rather, I want you to be informed both about what could happen by misusing Adderall and about what side effects you could experience as a result of taking Adderall. Now, it is vital to understand that these symptoms are drastically minimized when you take the prescription as prescribed. However, by taking it in excess or taking someone else's medication, you put yourself at an increased risk of side effects because you have no doctor monitoring your condition.

In order to understand the side effects that arise from taking Adderall, let's explore them together.

WHY DO MEDICATIONS HAVE SIDE EFFECTS?

It is a well-known fact that you should pay attention to the side effects of medications before you start taking them, but why do medications have side effects in the first place? Each medicine is developed in order to treat a particular medical issue, but they can have other unwanted effects, referred to as 'side effects' (What Are Side Effects and Why Do They Occur? | Guides | HIV I-Base, n.d.). Every drug has the potential to have a side effect, though oftentimes these side effects go unnoticed. In short, medications have side effects because the body is a complicated thing, and it is hard to make a medicine that only impacts one singular part of the body. Medications meant to target and resolve a headache can cause a headache if taken in excess, and the body does unpredictable things sometimes. As a result, something like an ADHD stimulant medication can cause completely or seemingly unrelated side effects. I'll dig a bit deeper into the reasoning surrounding this.

Both prescription medications and complementary medicines can cause side effects. Prescription medications can cause side effects, especially in correlation with other medications (Medicines and Side Effects, 2012). These are called 'interactions', and can occur between two prescriptions, OTC medications, and complementary medicines. Complementary medicines are also known as natural remedies, and are thought to be safer than medicine by many people. However, that is not the case at all. Some herbal medicines can act just as strongly on the body, causing undesirable side effects and powerful interactions as well. For example, certain herbs should never be used by pregnant individuals, as they can cause miscarriage.

It is also vital to know that complementary medications can interact with prescription ones, and that interaction is not always positive. This happens because some of the active ingredients in herbal remedies can be the same as active ingredients in prescription medications, increasing the impact of the medication on the body. Some of these ingredients can counteract each other as well. Either option will have the potential to produce undesirable effects. For example, St. John's wort increases the levels of serotonin in the brain. This sounds like a good thing, but in reality, this herb combined with an anti-depressant could cause serotonin toxicity, which is potentially deadly. Because of these potential interactions, it is important that you discuss any herbal remedies you currently, plan to, or are considering taking with your doctor before beginning either the prescription medication or the herbal medicine.

Moreover, the use of alcohol with certain medications can cause an increase in negative side effects. Drinking alcohol with medication can cause the medication to work harder or cause unwanted side effects. For example, if you drink with medication, you might experience excess dizziness. Blood pressure and nausea medication might not work after drinking alcohol, and when combined with stronger medication, alcohol can cause overdose. Because of these reasons, it is in your best interest to avoid drinking with your medication until you either consult a doctor or understand how the medication impacts you personally.

If you begin to experience side effects from your medication, you can call the emergency hotline in your area, consult your doctor or pharmacist, or visit the nearest emergency room. The best way to minimize side effects from medication is to take it exactly as prescribed and to avoid taking medication prescribed to someone else. These are all important things to keep in mind in order to stay safe while taking medication.

COMMON SIDE EFFECTS

There are tons of common side effects for Adderall, but this should be minimally concerning; most medications have very common side effects. These usually subside within a couple of weeks once your body becomes used to metabolizing the medication. If these systems persist for longer than two to six weeks, you should let your doctor know. Some of the common side effects associated with Adderall–many of which apply to similar medications as well–include (Llamas, 2023):

- Diarrhea
- Dizziness
- Dry mouth
- Fever
- Headache
- Insomnia
- Loss of appetite
- Mood swings
- Nausea
- Stomachache

No two people will experience the side effects of medication in the same way, just like no two bodies are quite the same. You might experience mostly stomach related side effects, whereas a friend might have headaches and insomnia. Because of this, it is important to keep track of symptoms as you start and continue any new medication. Moreover, it is important to keep in mind the other factors that impact the ability for you to experience side effects. According to the Food and Drug Administration, also known as the FDA, there are several bodily factors responsible for influencing the likelihood that you will experience side effects from a medication. Namely, your age, weight, body type, hormonal cycles, and any pre-existing conditions have the potential to impact the level of risk you face when it comes to side effects. Be sure to ask your doctor any questions you have about these side effects before starting or continuing to take your medication.

After hearing all of this, you might still be asking why these medications have these side effects. Isn't it a bit odd that a medication can cause both diarrhea and constipation as a side effect? It is! You're right. That boils down to how you react to different stimuli and your body's natural responses to the world around you. For example, the fight or flight response plays a major role in which side effects might manifest within you (Nall, 2019). As you may or may not know, the fight or flight response is a result of anxiety or fear. When you encounter these things, the body uses the norepinephrine and dopamine created by Adderall to allow you to have the ability to combat or flee from a terrifying situation. This is a protective mechanism that has kept human beings safe for centuries, but it is also a mechanism known for causing stomach problems. As a result, Adderall can impact your stomach and digestion in several ways.

When it comes to constipation, the effect is easily explained. In your gut, the hormones associated with the fight or flight response are known to push blood away. In other words, when your body and brain have been kicked into fight or flight mode, you are getting less blood flow to the parts of your stomach responsible for passing waste. This means that the blood vessels in your stomach can contract, resulting in constipation that is often associated with taking stimulant medications. This, in turn, can cause you to feel sick or nauseous, because your body is not operating as it normally does. Furthermore, Adderall and other stimulants have a strong potential to cause diarrhea as you adjust to the medication. This is because, at first, ADHD medications like Adderall can make you feel a tad bit anxious. Anxiety often leads to increased gastric activity, making you need to use the restroom. For people with stomach problems, stimulant medication can be especially troublesome.

SIDE EFFECTS IN CHILDREN

As you may have guessed, side effects differ a bit across age; therefore, kids and adults experience different side effects. Because children's bodies are smaller and more fragile than adults, plus the fact that their routines can be more easily disturbed, it is important that you take note of your child's habits in various areas so that you can compare their "normal" against a list of side effects (WebMD, 2016). If side effects give your child trouble, you can speak with your doctor about changing medication, dosage adjustments, and more.

One of the biggest issues parents have with Adderall is that it gives their child marked issues sleeping, which is also a common side effect in adults. The stimulating effect is known to keep them up at night, no matter the age, and especially in the body of a small child, this effect can take hold. Furthermore, these problems tend to be strongest when the medication is first started. The best way to combat this side effect is to make sure your child takes their medication as early in the day as possible. You can also switch from an extended-release medication to a standard release medication by asking your doctor about it. Standard release medication will wear off before your child's head hits the pillow, making it far easier for them to rest at night. Another alternative is non-stimulant ADHD medications, which can be taken at bedtime as they have a mild sedating effect. Paying attention to how these medications impact your child's sleep will allow you to effectively avoid sleep-related side effects as best you can.

It is also possible that your child complains of headaches, stomach aches, or nausea as a result of taking their medication. This is a side effect that both adults and children face. Fortunately, these side effects go away relatively quickly after the body gets used to the medication, but if your child is having a lot of trouble with it, there's something you can do to potentially lessen this nasty side effect. Try feeding your child with their medication. For example, providing them with their medication about halfway through breakfast might allow the medication to rest more easily in their small stomach, creating less issues like stomach aches and nausea. This works for adults too and is a safe way to take stimulant medications if they cause digestion-related issues. Once the medication has had a week or so to settle into your child's system, you can try giving it to them without food once again to see if it still upsets their stomach. If it does so even with food, let your child's doctor know. A treatment change may be in order.

Once your child begins Adderall or a similar medication, you might notice that they do not want to eat very much for a while after taking their medication, as this is a common effect that results from stimulating medications. If this effect persists, do not worry just yet—try feeding them a nutritious breakfast before giving them their medication, allowing for a small lunch and large dinner in accordance with when the medication wears off in the evening. If you notice that your child is losing weight, then you should talk to your doctor about the effects of the medication.

Irritability and mood changes may also arise as a result of starting a stimulant medication. This especially takes effect after the medication wears off, which is about four hours for standard release and 12 for extended release. Once the medication wears off, they might have something called a 'rebound period', where they have a poor attitude or low motivation. This often occurs around the time they might eat dinner or go to bed for the evening. One of the best things you can do to counteract this effect is to plan your evening activities so that nothing frustrating occurs during rebound time. Perhaps give your child something to do that they enjoy, or wait until after the rebound period for obligations like homework to take place. Otherwise, if you can't figure out a scheduling situation to ease these effects, consider letting your doctor know. They may prescribe a fast, but short-acting, short-lived dose of their medication for evenings to allow the rebound period to dissipate.

Additionally, stopping your child's ADHD medication can result in fainting or dizziness, especially if they take a non-stimulant medication. This is because non-stimulant medications lower the heart rate and blood pressure. On its own, that can result in dizziness and fainting, but if the medication is stopped suddenly, their blood pressure may spike, causing further health complications. If you want your child to stop taking medication, talk to your doctor and mention that you are having concerns about their medication. Taking them off their medication without medical consultation may have an extreme negative effect on their health.

Finally, some parents express concerns that stimulant medications, like Adderall, have the ability to impact their child's physical growth. The reason that many people think Adderall and similar medications can impact both the height and weight of children is due to the appetite loss and dopamine boost. This is because height and weight are interlinked and dopamine can slow growth hormone in excess. However, others theorize that this effect might be caused by ADHD medication's ability to target metabolic rates within the body and affect a child's growth that way. Fortunately, the research surrounding this difficult and tumultuous side effect has declared that any effects may be temporary. Besides that, the behavior improvements likely outweigh these temporary effects on your child's growth. If you are concerned about the rate at which your child is growing, be sure to let your child's doctor know. It is likely that the doctor has already been monitoring their growth, and on your end, there are some things that you can do. For instance, you can include more nutrient-rich foods or energy-boosting foods in your kid's diet to try and counteract this effect.

SIDE EFFECTS OF ADDERALL XR

As it turns out, Adderall extended release, also called 'Adderall XR', has its very own side effects that are present in the extended-release formula of this medication. Adderall XR has a lot of similar side effects to the standard release formula, it is true, but some are a bit notable and different and should be made note of. It is important to understand the differences in how two formulas of the same medication will impact the body of you or your child. Many people do wonder if the different formulas differ in side effects. The answer to that question is "yes, but not by much." Some of the common side effects that arise from Adderall XR include weight loss, stomach aches, dizziness, nausea, diarrhea, and insomnia (Adderall XR Oral: Uses, Side Effects, Interactions, Pictures, Warnings & Dosing - WebMD, n.d.). As you can see, this list is strikingly familiar to that of the side effects of standard release Adderall; however, Adderall XR has symptoms like fever and nervousness that are more likely to accompany the extended-release formula of this medication. As with any version of medication, be sure to monitor your side effects and let your doctor know if they become severe or persist.

SERIOUS SIDE EFFECTS OF ADDERALL

In addition to the common side effects of Adderall mentioned so far, Adderall has a slew of more serious side effects that are truly nothing to ignore. The serious side effects of Adderall can range from mild to life threatening, and as such, it is vital that you know what these side effects are. While rare, these side effects have been reported in conjunction with patients who took Adderall actively, so it is important to keep these things in mind and know what to watch for.

For example, one serious side effect that is not necessarily life threatening, but can disturb your day greatly, is the rebound effect. We talked about the rebound effect briefly regarding ADHD stimulant medication and children, but what about in adults or when the rebound is serious? ADHD rebound from medication occurs when the medication wears off, and it is a quite normal reaction when more influential medications wear off (Rodden, 2019). Rebound presents itself as a myriad of ADHD symptoms occurring all at once the medication leaves the system. Typically, rebound will last for about an hour. It occurs in those who metabolize the medication rather quickly, and the symptoms of rebound can vary. Serious side effects from rebound are rare, but can include anything from behavioral issues to health issues like vomiting, dizziness, tiredness, blood pressure changes, etc.

In addition, there is such a thing as an Adderall overdose, and it should be watched for carefully as an overdose of Adderall can be potentially life threatening. Unfortunately, it may be difficult to spot an Adderall overdose at first, but there are several symptoms to look out for that can key you in on if yourself or others have overdosed on their medication (Patterson, 2022). There are both mental and physical symptoms that accompany such a thing. First, watch out for symptoms like confusion or restlessness. If someone exhibits these signs more than normal, they may be experiencing an Adderall overdose. Things like depression, elevated panic, hallucinations, and violence might be signs you notice as well. Furthermore, along with those symptoms, someone might be breathing fast or hyperventilating, shaking, dizzy, nauseous, or have a fever or quick heartbeat. In very severe cases, someone might faint, have a seizure or heart attack, etc.

An Adderall overdose can easily lead to someone's untimely death. As such, it is important to understand what to do in the event that you or someone you know overdoses on their medication. When someone is experiencing an Adderall overdose, either call your local emergency number or take them to the emergency room as fast as possible. Only medical professionals know how to appropriately treat an overdose of Adderall because there is no medication that prevents or stops it. Instead, the medical professionals will need to treat the signs of the overdose. Getting the person who is having an overdose care immediately is crucial to saving their life.

There are also some severe cardiovascular side effects that may result from Adderall as well. Adderall can raise your heart rate and blood pressure alike, which can also contribute to you breathing more harshly (Cristol, 2022). These symptoms usually subside after stopping the medication, although doing so abruptly can cause opposite yet just as severe cardiovascular side effects. The main purpose of informing you of such risks is to encourage you to let your doctor know if you suffer from high blood pressure or heart conditions/issues prior to beginning a stimulant medication.

Psychiatric side effects may accompany the use of Adderall as well. Mental health conditions like schizophrenia and psychosis can be worsened by taking Adderall. Furthermore, you may experience heightened levels of psychosis or suicidal thoughts when taking Adderall fi you have a history of mental illness.

Furthermore, Adderall does put you at a heightened risk for something called 'peripheral vasculopathy'. Peripheral vasculopathy involves a circulatory issue wherein blood vessels are narrowed and allow for less blood flow to the limbs. This disease can cause numbness, weakness, or cold temperatures in lower extremities, among other things. Recent studies have shown that there may be a connection between peripheral vasculopathy and those who take Adderall XR, as it is thought that Adderall XR results in arterial spasms (Hritani et al., 2015). When taking Adderall XR, in order to avoid any potential arterial complications, it is important to monitor how your body feels both before and after you started taking the medication. Any concerns should be escalated to your doctor as soon as possible.

Raynaud's phenomenon may also accompany the use of Adderall. This is an incredibly rare side effect, but one to watch out for nonetheless. Raynaud's phenomenon is something that occurs involving the blood vessels (Gordon, 2015). It causes them to react to cold or stress in a particular way, usually with them constricting or otherwise responding in a non-typical way that they should not behave in. This can be observed most closely in the fingers or toes and is characterized by the coloring of these body parts turning to red, blue, or white. It is estimated that between three and 20 percent of the population have this condition. There is often no cause for this condition, but medications like Adderall can worsen it, especially in people who already have this condition. In other words, it is likely that if someone already has Raynaud's, it will worsen when taking Adderall. The cold and emotional distress are the biggest triggers for symptoms of Raynaud's, which means caution should be taken to stay warm in the wintertime.

A final serious side effect that can result from using Adderall–or, primarily, misusing it–is serotonin syndrome. Serotonin syndrome might not sound like a bad thing because serotonin is the "happy chemical" after all. However, serotonin syndrome is one of the most dangerous side effects any medication can have. Serotonin syndrome occurs when there is too much serotonin being released in the brain, which causes the body to be unable to function properly (Serotonin Syndrome – Adderall and Serotonin, 2018). Common symptoms of serotonin syndrome include:

- Confusion
- Agitation
- Sweating
- Problems with coordination
- Nausea and vomiting

- Headaches
- Changes in blood pressure
- Changes in body temperature
- Digestive problems
- Sweating
- Depression
- Kidney damage
- Seizures
- Changes in heart rate
- Loss of consciousness
- Death

Serotonin syndrome requires immediate medical attention; otherwise, the risk of someone dying is high. It is treated by medical professionals based on the severity of the condition. Stomach pumping or other methods may be used to stop the medication from doing more harm, or other methods may be employed. Serotonin syndrome is the result of either an overdose of a medication or an unfortunate interaction between two or more substances. As such, it is vital that all instructions provided by your doctor are followed closely.

Once again, I'd like to restate that the serious side effects of Adderall are rare. These side effects are by no means anticipated or expected for people who take Adderall, but knowing that there is a potential for something to occur can save lives, including your own or your child's life.

LONG-TERM EFFECTS OF ADDERALL

Several long-term effects are associated with taking Adderall as well, and it is good to be mindful of them. Before starting a stimulant medication, it is important to understand how it can impact you in the long run, as this can influence your physical and mental health as well as the wellbeing of those around you. Most of the long-term symptoms dissipate as soon as the medication is stopped, but some can remain for a lifetime. It is crucial that you understand the risks you may encounter before starting this medication.

Symptoms of irritability, anger, or aggression, for example, may persist as long as the medication is being taken. Adderall contributes to the level of these emotions because it controls hormones and other bodily chemicals found within the brain. For example, dopamine is responsible for motivation and is one of the hormones impacted by the use of a medication like Adderall (Kashyap, 2022). But if the dose is too high or the body never becomes familiar with the excess dopamine being triggered, the extra dopamine can cause aggression or a decline in impulse control. Likewise, the norepinephrine hormone controlled by

Adderall can be impacted. This hormone controls alertness, and when Adderall is taken, this can increase the level of anxiety one feels. Moreover, serotonin is the pleasure chemical in our brain, yet heightened levels of it can cause agitation. Adderall usually helps quell emotional symptoms brought on by ADHD, but in some cases, it can worsen them. This usually indicates that the medication needs to be altered in some way, be it type or dosage. Usually, once the patient stops taking Adderall, these symptoms will subside, so there is no need to worry about this persisting indefinitely.

Changes in mood and behavior may also arise long-term as a result of taking Adderall. This is because of the similar impact it has on happiness-creating hormones in the brain. In rare cases, people who take Adderall report feeling sluggish and depressed as a result of doing so, which seems like the exact opposite of what should be occurring. For some individuals, the solution is as simple as switching to a different stimulant medication. For others, an anti-depressant may be added to help balance out the effect of the medication. It depends on the individual and the specific reason why the Adderall resulted in lowered mood and depressive behavior in the first place.

In addition, sexual problems, including but not limited to erectile dysfunction, may arise as a result of taking

Adderall, and may persist even after the body is used to metabolizing the medication (The Medical Info on How Adderall Impacts Your Sex Drive, n.d.). This is because amphetamines, the main ingredient in stimulant ADHD medications, lower the production of testosterone which can result in lowered sexual performance. Fortunately, these symptoms dissipate once the effect of the medication has worn off.

Hallucinations are a final long-term symptom of Adderall and similar stimulant medications that we haven't mentioned thus far. This is because using Adderall frequently over time can cause what is referred to as 'substance-induced psychosis' (Adderall & Psychosis, Paranoia | How Does Adderall Affect People with Psychosis?, 2022). When you start taking Adderall, there is a low, but present, possibility that you trigger a psychotic disorder's onset of psychosis more generally. Symptoms of Adderall psychosis include:

- Lack of concentration
- Delusions
- Increased motor activity
- Disorganized thoughts
- Anxiety
- Hallucinations
- Lethargy
- Violent behavior

- Socially withdrawn
- Paranoia

Furthermore, something called 'Adderall paranoia' may be triggered, resulting in the following side effects:

- Mistrust
- Extreme cautiousness
- Defensive attitude
- Inability to relax
- Argumentative mindset

The fortunate news is that while this can be scary, most cases resolve within days. Some cases can last for years, but in those cases, the potential that someone already had a psychiatric disorder is high. If you are already at risk or have a disorder like schizophrenia or another disorder that has a main symptom of psychosis, let your doctor know before beginning Adderall or any other stimulant medication.

Of course, other symptoms may persist into the long-term, such as gastrointestinal issues and insomnia mentioned earlier; however, these usually stop once the medication has stopped. If these symptoms continue on after a few weeks of taking your medication, let your doctor know, and they will identify some treatment deviations that might help your situation.

CHAPTER SUMMARY

- Side effects common to Adderall include nausea, vomiting, weight loss, headaches, and more.
- It is important to watch out for these side effects in yourself or your child.
- Children experience a unique array of side effects when taking ADHD medication, and it is important to understand these to keep your child safe.
- Adderall XR and SR have very similar side effects.
- There are also a wide variety of serious and long-term effects of Adderall, including overdose, addiction, and more.

Overall, understanding all of the potential symptoms of Adderall is what's going to keep you safe. As I mentioned at the beginning of this chapter, misusing Adderall has been a major issue in recent years, with large numbers of people—both children and adults—taking Adderall that wasn't prescribed to them. You might have noticed that addiction was a suspiciously absent long-term effect of taking medications like Adderall. That's not because I forgot about it; rather, the addiction and black-market issues surrounding Adderall consumption are such a major proponent of side effects and issues with Adderall that it will be the entire focus of our next chapter.

5

ADDICTION AND BLACK-MARKET ISSUES

Quitting smoking is easy. I have done it a hundred times. –Mark Twain

The unfortunate fact about Adderall is that, when misused, it is an incredibly addictive substance. There are so many stories about lives that have been ruined due to an Adderall addiction that stemmed from misusing Adderall. For example, one mother of two from Arizona revealed that, in 2015, she became addicted to Adderall (Johnston, 2019). She was initially prescribed the drug for her ADHD, but after she started losing weight from the medication, she became addicted to it. She visited a doctor to get help for the condition, but that was only after losing years of valuable time with her children.

There are a few things to think about when it comes to unfortunate cases like these. First, we do not know for sure how she was taking her medication, but it definitely wasn't being closely monitored by a doctor. Second, how educated was she on the side effects and risks associated with Adderall? My guess is not very, and that is not really her fault–in 2015, the education available surrounding this topic was limited. Situations like this one sadden me greatly, but they're worth learning from. With the power of education about addiction and side effects of medication, together we can minimize the potential for addiction and a further perpetuation of black market selling of drugs like Adderall; ones that have the power to change lives for better or for worse.

Now let me be clear—the intention of this chapter is not to scare you or to talk about how "big pharma" is terrible. The intention of this chapter is to shine light on terrible situations that can occur if you become addicted to Adderall, take it in a way that it is not prescribed, etc., as well as how distribution and selling of Adderall contributes to addiction and floods the markets with danger. I cannot stress enough or strongly enough that you should only use Adderall as prescribed and refuse to buy or sell Adderall on the black market. In order to further educate you on the subject, let's first talk about how Adderall became something of a "study drug".

ADDERALL AS A STUDY DRUG

Adderall has been widely known as a "study drug" for a few years due to its propensity to allow those who take it to focus. If you are not familiar with the term 'study drug', let me catch you up briefly. Study drugs are prescription stimulant medications, including but not limited to Adderall, which are abused by people (typically in college) to enhance mental functioning (Study Drug Facts, History and Statistics | Dangers and Legality, 2023). It is taken for memory, focus, alertness, and attention, but it is also commonly taken by people to whom it is not prescribed. Adderall being used as a study drug is a massive problem, and one study in 2016 indicated that Adderall abuse increased by over 67% (Recovery, 2022). That's a staggering number of people taking and potentially becoming addicted to a medication just to stay up late and study or write a paper.

The use of Adderall as a study drug might seem like something that is not a big deal to you. Something I have heard a lot is, "So what? It helps them focus and do their schoolwork." But the reality of it is that most of the people–especially students–who abuse Adderall are doing so due to systemic pressure, not because they need the medication. In order to further enumerate upon this point, I'll explain a bit about Adderall addiction and how it impacts people.

ADDERALL ADDICTION

Before we can talk about what Adderall abuse looks like, we should talk about what Adderall abuse is. Adderall abuse can present itself in many ways, depending on the individual abusing the drug. One way that Adderall abuse can manifest is by someone taking a higher dose than prescribed (Patterson, 2023). This can look like a few things. Someone who has an Adderall prescription might take their medication in excess for a few days, then not take it at all the following days, or someone who is prescribed Adderall could purchase excess Adderall off the black market in order to abuse the drug. Both of these are common, yet inappropriate, uses of Adderall, even though the person in question had a prescription. Another manifestation of Adderall abuse is taking it any way except for orally, including by snorting it. Furthermore, people often abuse Adderall by taking it for non-medicinal purposes, taking it more often than prescribed, taking someone else's prescription, or by purchasing it from an illegal

source. All of these things qualify as abuse of the drug–
and of most drugs, as a matter of fact.

In 2015, 7% of college students in the United States
reported using Adderall for non-medical purposes.
That might not sound like a lot, but that amounts to
over 1.4 million students who admitted to misusing
Adderall. That's just in one year, and does not account
for those who didn't admit to using the drug nor for
those older or younger than 18-22. That's absolutely
jarring. Over a million people misuse Adderall each
year, and nearly as many have an addiction to the
substance as a result of misuse, even if they do not
know it. Regarding addiction of any kind, and especially Adderall addiction, there are a few signs to look
for in order to identify it. These symptoms include:

- Headache
- Dry mouth
- Hoarseness
- Nausea
- Upset stomach
- Digestive issues
- Lowered appetite
- Diarrhea or constipation
- Anxiety
- Restlessness
- Fast heartbeat

- Difficulty sleeping
- Excessive fatigue
- Changes in sex drive

If you notice someone you know exhibiting these symptoms, it might be a good idea to sit them down and talk to them about what's going on. In a minute, we will discuss Adderall addiction treatment options which can help you find help for someone in need.

Beyond that, there's also something called 'Adderall dependence' that differs a bit from Adderall addiction. You can become both addicted and dependent upon Adderall. Adderall dependence is a natural psychological response, and it can frequently occur to people who take Adderall in a healthy way (Gorman, 2022). It most often manifests as a physical dependence instead of a mental one. This is not the same as an addiction. Physically, your body might seem like it needs your medication to function, but when you have a dependence on a medication, you will not obsess over it. That's the defining characteristic separating dependence from addiction. To wean you from an Adderall dependence, your doctor will simply taper your dosage. As I mentioned, dependence is normal and very common. Signs of dependence on Adderall include:

- Inability to concentrate without Adderall

- Fatigue when use is ceased
- Weight loss
- Sleep deprivation
- Anxiety
- Heightened focus
- Excess energy

On the other hand, Adderall addiction is more serious. Addiction requires dependence as a prerequisite, but not all dependence becomes an addiction. After someone becomes dependent on a drug, they will either remain that way throughout the duration of treatment, or they will spiral into an addiction due to unhealthy habits regarding how they take their medication. Addiction is dependence with further associated behaviors. Once taken off of the medication, an addict will do whatever they can and make it their primary goal to obtain more Adderall. They will, if prescribed the medication, run out early as a result of taking way more than necessary and will do whatever they can to obtain more, even if it means doing so illegally. Obsessive cravings for your medication are often considered to be a sign of addiction.

TREATMENT AND RELAPSE PREVENTION

Unfortunately, Adderall addiction is incredibly common, but that also means that treatments and relapse prevention options for addicts are also common, which is the silver lining to it all. If you or someone you know finds themselves addicted to Adderall, this section is dedicated to informing you about treatment options and relapse prevention in order to get you healthy once again. Everyone deserves help, and I in no way want to make you or anyone else feel bad for an addiction. You deserve help, and anyone you know who struggles with addiction does too.

When it comes to rehabilitation treatment for drug addiction, there are often two options—inpatient and outpatient, and both are available for Adderall addiction (Adderall Addiction Treatment, n.d.). Inpatient treatment involves admitting yourself to a hospital or other treatment center where you will essentially live for several weeks. Inpatient care is often the precursor for outpatient care, which means that before outpatient care is an option, you will have to go to a rehabilitation center. This is the safest way to do so because medical professionals will be available around the clock to assist in your recovery. As you recover, it is going to be instrumental that you address the cause of your addiction, whether it is trauma, mental health issues, or other complications within your life. You have to address what made you begin the addiction in the first place in order to avoid continuing it.

As far as an inpatient program goes, they offer comprehensive treatments aimed at facilitating long-term recovery. Most programs last at least 30 days, though depending on your needs, the program may last longer. In fact, many programs allow you to stay until you personally feel comfortable enough to exit into outpatient care. Not all programs do, though, so it is important that you look for a program that supports your particular needs and ideal treatment options. In addition to a plan that allows you to stay for an ideal amount of time, different programs employ different methods for recovery. For instance, some centers use a 12-step model for recovery while others use cognitive behavioral therapy. Whatever it may be, you will also spend plenty of time with others in the same situation as well as one-on-one with a therapist in inpatient care.

This brings me to describing outpatient treatment. Outpatient treatment often comes after inpatient or is conducted on its own in various stages, which are usually called 'levels' within treatment. The first level is referred to as a 'partial hospitalization program'. This is where you attend all-day treatment at a facility, but you do not live in that facility. People opt to live at home or in a sober living facility to keep them accountable. The treatment you receive during a partial hospitalization is very similar to residential, combining group, individual, and holistic approaches to recovery. The only major difference is that you do not sleep at the facility. Level two involves something called an 'intensive outpatient program'. This is where you attend treatment at an addiction treatment center part time, meeting three to five times a week for a few hours at a time. These are usually group therapy based, helping you connect with others and remain accountable. The third and final level involves an outpatient program, where you only attend outpatient treatment for a couple of hours one day a week. This is often a preferable option for people who can't afford or do not feel comfortable in a full-time inpatient facility, or people who have a less severe or short-term addiction.

There are also a myriad of therapeutic options available for treating Adderall addiction. These options might be used in inpatient, outpatient, or on their own. Individual therapy is the first kind of therapy you might encounter. It is a one-on-one session between you and your therapist where you can talk about your addiction, things that caused your hospitalization, and more. In individual therapy, you will learn how to cope with things that led to your addiction as well as how to prevent relapse. Individual therapy is a valuable part of treating addiction and maintaining your sobriety in the long run. You will also engage in group therapy. During group therapy, you will engage with others who also struggle with addiction. Depending on where you receive treatment, this will involve people with the same or different addictions from you. Mostly, during group therapy, you share stories and support to create a network of support for recovery.

Something called 'cognitive behavioral therapy' may be employed on its own or in combination with individual or group therapies. Cognitive behavioral therapy helps you identify and alter the thoughts and behaviors which drive your addiction. It is a short-term form of therapy that is long-term effective, which is one of the major reasons it is used so often. CBT is a very effective way to permanently eliminate thoughts and behaviors that contribute toward making your life more difficult.

You might also be invited to attend family therapy, during which you will have the opportunity to mend relationships that were damaged as a result of your addiction. They will also help you improve the communication between members of your family.

Finally, holistic therapy may be involved in your treatment plan. Holistic therapies involve creative methods for resolving addiction related problems, including art, yoga, drama, and more.

Once you have finished the formal steps of treatment, addiction does not just go away. It is an unfortunate aspect and issue that once you have done so much work, you are still left with a lifelong battle. Fortunately, however, there are ways to combat cravings and maintain your rehabilitated state, avoiding relapse and further addiction. One of the best ways to prevent relapse is Adderall rehab aftercare. Rehab aftercare is continued services that take place after substance abuse treatment ends in order to prevent you from relapsing (Adderall Addiction Aftercare and Relapse Prevention, n.d.). It helps with avoiding drugs and refusing drugs if offered, managing cravings, and managing stress. Relapse prevention is a type of aftercare strategy that helps prevent or delay the use of whatever drug you were addicted to; in this case, Adderall.

One of the biggest issues people have with staying clean after rehabilitation involves cravings. Cravings are strong urges to engage in substance abuse, intrusive thoughts about relapsing, having the inability to think about anything other than your source of addiction, or prolonged distress from thinking about your source of addiction (End Adderall Cravings, Prevent Relapse and Find Help, n.d.). These cravings are one of the biggest reasons that people relapse. Cravings are often a result of triggers. Drug cravings, and cravings for Adderall specifically, can last for different lengths depending on things like a person's genetics, mental health, and more.

Triggers can come in many forms. For example, thoughts and emotions can fill someone with the desire to start taking a substance again. Any intrusive thought or strong emotion might remind the person of the mindset they were in when they took the drug. Additionally, being in physical pain or discomfort can bring about an overwhelming feeling of needing to relapse in order to alleviate that physical discomfort. Avoiding situations that cause physical discomfort is often desirable, but many therapeutic practices encourage not avoiding the situations, but instead developing coping mechanisms to handle them. Another common trigger involves being reminded of the drug abuse, whether that is an environment or physically seeing drug paraphernalia. Being in environments or with people who used drugs together can trigger a relapse as well as seeing something like someone take pills. It can be a very triggering situation for any recovering/recovered addict.

It is unfortunate, but relapse is common for those who were previously addicted to stimulants like Adderall. Therefore, it is important to understand what triggers one to use Adderall or other drugs. This allows you to avoid situations that can potentially be triggering.

ADDERALL SHORTAGE

If you currently take Adderall or pay attention to the news, you may already know that there has been an ongoing shortage of Adderall in the United States. This occurred shortly after many people across the country experienced significant issues with getting refills for the medication filled. The Food and Drug Administration eventually confirmed that the shortage was due to a shortage of the immediate release amphetamine mixed salts, which are what is used to create Adderall. Teva, the company that produces Adderall, has said that part of the reason behind this shortage is that, lately, a rise in Adderall prescriptions has caused backorders and necessitated increased production levels. This has been causing intermittent shortages of Adderall, both brand name and generic, throughout the United States.

As you can probably tell, this puts a major cramp in the ability of people with ADHD who take Adderall to get treated for their condition. What exactly are the effects of such a shortage? One person reported that in light of the Adderall shortage, she has started taking her friend's medication, which is not her prescription (Knibbs, 2022). They're a higher dosage and might even be too high. Because of situations like this, people are worrying that the Adderall shortage could be potentially deadly as people are turning to more and more barbaric and illegal means to get the medications that they so desperately need. Adderall is a very important medication that people rely on to function properly within our society. Without it, people are left with anything from severe withdrawal symptoms to feeling forced to purchase pills off the black market. In fact, some sources report that people are turning to black market stimulants as a substitute.

This has major, negative implications. This could result in people turning en masse to black market solutions, rapidly removing themselves from the pharmaceutical market. Some say that the resemblance of this shift to the opioid crisis is uncanny. This also has major implications for the black market itself. People are unprepared to stop their medication at the drop of the hat, meaning some will, in desperation, turn to unregulated sale sources for medication. This is something that can easily kill thousands of people because the black market is entirely unregulated. We will talk more about the black market and sales of medication and drugs through it in a few moments.

So, how can you cope with the Adderall shortage in the meantime? Well, whatever you do, do not think you need to resort to illicit means to get your medication or a lousy substitute full of god knows what. Instead, if you can't get your prescription filled, call your doctor. Your doctor can find out more information about what the pharmacy has that can be used to deal with getting you a different type of Adderall or a different medication altogether to tide you over until the shortage ends and production catches up with demands. Furthermore, if you are currently taking Adderall, it is okay to lower your dose or take a break from your medication if you feel safe to do so in order to save medication in case you struggle to get it refilled. Moreover, you can consider a different formulation of Adderall that is in less demand by either taking a different stimulant, extended-release medication, or something else. Your doctor will be able to discuss these options with you.

BLACK MARKET SALES

What is the black market anyway? The black market is not really one market. It is more like a network of places and means through which people sell things illegally and without government involvement. There's no taxation involved and no regulation either. It is kind of like someone three states away offering to sell you drugs if you pass an envelope of money through a bunch of people to them, and then when you get the drugs, they're either not what you wanted or could kill you. There are virtually no safety measures in place, and it is not worth the risk at all. There are, however, unique risks that accompany purchasing medication through black market channels. After hearing these reasons, I hope you will be completely dissuaded from engaging with any black-market activity.

For example, one reason that medication should not be purchased online through these avenues is that the medication is not monitored by a healthcare professional. This is atrocious for two reasons. First, the lack of medical monitoring puts you at severe risk of health issues, especially with medications like Adderall. This is because you have no one helping you with dosages. You could take far too much and cause an overdose, serotonin syndrome, or worse–death, just by trying to help yourself out. Moreover, you will not even know if Adderall is the right medication for you. Beyond that, Adderall comes with potential complications like high blood pressure that a black-market salesperson does not care if you have or could die from. Second, what you purchase might not even be Adderall. No one is ensuring that things sold on the black market are what you are being told they are. Someone could sell you "Adderall" and send you anything from Aspirin to fentanyl. It is a risk that is not worth being taken.

Another reason you should not do this involves self-diagnosing. Self-diagnosing occurs when someone decides that they have a condition based on research they've done on their own. This research may be extensive or not, but the bottom line is that you are not a medical professional with the capacity to diagnose something, especially ADHD. Doing so and then purchasing black market medications can put your life and the safety of those around you at risk. You should avoid selling or giving away your medication or purchasing anything on the black market for this very reason.

CHAPTER SUMMARY

- Adderall became a study drug people used to benefit them before exams.
- Adderall is not a bad medication, but it is important to only take it as prescribed and to avoid reselling or purchasing from someone other than a pharmacy.
- Failure to do so can cause addiction.
- Treatment for addiction comes in the form of both inpatient and outpatient, and outpatient treatment has three levels.
- The Adderall shortage impacts both those who buy Adderall legally and illegally.

- Black market purchases put your life at risk. You should not sell or purchase anything over the black market.

This chapter focused itself on addiction and the black market pertaining to Adderall and its consumption. You now understand how Adderall addiction differs from dependence, what is involved in the treatment of Adderall addiction, what the Adderall shortage is, why it occurred and how to survive despite it, and why black-market sales of Adderall are bad. After this chapter, it should go without saying that the misuse of Adderall—especially as a study drug or by those who are not prescribed it—is never a good idea. The associated health risks can cause complications beyond measure. After reading about everything associated with ADHD and Adderall as a medication, you may or may not be coming to the conclusion that Adderall is not for you, or perhaps you are just curious about the other options available. Whatever the case may be, the next chapter is for you. In the next chapter, we will talk about managing ADHD without the use of medication.

6

MANAGING ADHD AND ADD
WITHOUT MEDICATION

When making a decision of minor importance, I have
always found it advantageous to consider all the pros
and cons. –Sigmund Freud

If you've read this far, I think you're capable of considering everything I've said and making your own decision regarding whether or not ADHD medication is for you. Personally, I think that Adderall is a miracle-working medication that changes lives, but I also recognize that it's not for everyone. With that being said, I believe that if you've read this far and have decided that medication is not for you, then that's your right, and I applaud you for making such a sound, yet open minded, decision. In light of that decision, or in case you've decided to try natural/non-medication related solutions first, this chapter will cover various options for treating ADHD that have nothing to do with medication. It is my belief that for some people, treating ADHD without medication is possible and realistic. So, if you've decided to go that route, then this chapter is for you.

Regarding scientific evidence of treatments for ADHD that aren't medication, some have been effective and some have not. There is little evidence–for instance–that supplements help with ADHD, but there's strong evidence suggesting sleep, diet, and routines can help with ADHD. In my opinion, whatever works... works! Even if there's no science to back it up, if you personally find it beneficial to your own life, then do it, so long as it's safe.

TO MEDICATE OR NOT

How do you make the decision whether or not to medicate yourself? How do you know whether or not it is a good idea to medicate your child? There are some methods and ways to determine how you feel about medication and if it's the right option for you. For example, there are some questions you should ask yourself before beginning treatment for yourself or your child. Some of those questions can include things like (ADHD: To Medicate or Not to Medicate?, 2021):

- What kind of medication is it going to be?
- What time and what frequency will this medication be taken with?
- What are the most common side effects that I can anticipate to experience?
- Can the medication cause any interference with my daily life?

In addition, a good piece of advice to keep in mind is that you should not start any medication unless you feel like you are well informed about it. Now that you've read so far into this book, you are definitely well informed enough to begin taking Adderall if you so choose and discuss it with your doctor.

Beyond that, there are a couple of other things to consider. For instance, once you start medication, every few months you should take time to reflect on if it's the right decision for you. Make sure that the benefits are outweighing any side effects, and that you're enjoying life on the medication. Moreover, you might not know this but just because someone starts a stimulant medication does not mean that they will need to take it for their entire life. In other words, after you and your doctor evaluate how treatment is going, you might make the decision to go off of your meds entirely. This can work and leave you feeling fine afterwards because sometimes medication has the ability to "fix" or permanently alter our mental state. This results in medication continuing to work even when it's no longer in the body.

Something else you should ensure is that you are making the decisions for your own or your child's treatment first and foremost. If, at any point, it begins to feel like your doctor has taken the lead in your treatment or is making decisions you don't really feel comfortable with, then it's time to speak up and advocate for yourself. You don't have to take or do anything you don't want yourself to do, and the best treatment plans are ones guided by you anyway.

Overall, the decision on whether or not to medicate yourself is completely yours and yours alone. You should consider if the medication will benefit you and what those benefits are, as well as periodically evaluate if your medication is still benefiting you as your treatment progresses.

ALTERNATIVE TREATMENTS

The first of the many alternative treatment options I have for you involves supplementation. Starting medication or starting your child on medication can be very daunting and the side effects can be more anxiety inducing than it's worth. Instead, you can look to nutritional supplements to try and alleviate some symptoms of ADHD. Nutritional supplements are supplements that provide basic nutrients that you might not get from your food, allowing you to feel and function better (Newmark, 2019). Many people have reported that ADHD symptoms seem to subside when treated with a combination of supplements, so my goal is to provide you with various supplements that you can try.

One option is omega-3 fatty acids. These are usually obtained through fish oil and studies have indicated that this supplement might benefit the brain in terms of attention and impulsivity. The details are a bit murky on how much and what kind of omega-3 fatty acids to take despite the ample research on them. The most important ones, as indicated by folks with ADHD, include EPA and DHA. People with ADHD have generally recommended that, in combination, children should take 1,000mg of the supplement whereas older people should take up to 2,000. Additionally, it is recommended that there be two times as much EPA as DHA for the treatment to be effective.

These fatty acids work to improve brain function because they are necessary for brain function in the first place. EPA and DHA contribute to the function and development in the brain, and both seem to play a role in the functioning of a brain throughout life as well as the development of it in babies (Pearson, 2017). In studies on animals, the ones fed diets without omega-3 fatty acids exhibited lower levels of learning and memory. Furthermore, it has been shown that fish oil and similar sources of omega-3 can benefit memory loss, concentration, focus, and other aspects of brain function that those with ADHD often have trouble with. One of the best things about fish oil is that it has very few cons explaining why you should not include it in your diet. So, if you think it might help, give omega-3s a try!

Another supplement you can try for ADHD is zinc. Zinc is especially useful for children with ADHD. There has been a bit of positive research showing that taking zinc with a stimulant medication makes less of the stimulant necessary for optimal functioning. The amount of zinc someone needs a day does vary, so if you plan to start taking a zinc supplement, I would recommend consulting your doctor first. However, 20-25mg is typically safe for a child without any blood work, so it should be safe for you as well. Zinc is beneficial because it allows for better communication within the brain and allows the brain to be more engaged as well. This helps with memory and learning that people with ADHD often struggle with.

There are many pros and cons to consider when it comes to any supplement, and zinc is no exception. I'll start us off with the pros. First, zinc is available over the counter. This is a fantastic benefit, considering things like Adderall are not available over the counter. Instead, taking something like zinc that is more accessible, but can leave you with the same benefits, might be a great option. Another valuable pro that supports the use of zinc is that it's cheap. Name brand bottles can run you some money, but generic zinc medications can cost as low as one dollar. This is an exceptional reason to consider taking a zinc supplement because it's far cheaper than prescription medication in the first place. Finally, zinc is safe for those who are pregnant, which is a concern for people who are pregnant and taking Adderall. Many people wonder how stimulant medications might affect their baby in utero, but with zinc the risk is null.

On the other hand, there are some cons to consider. First, too much zinc can cause stomach problems, much like Adderall can. If you opted for supplements to avoid the associated stomach issues, then zinc as your supplement of choice probably isn't the way to go. Zinc can result in constipation or diarrhea, as well as nausea and vomiting. If you do want to take zinc despite this, however, taking it with food should alleviate some of these symptoms. The downside of this is that your body absorbs far less of the zinc if you take it with food. Because of this, it's best to take your zinc supplement on an empty stomach. My final con for you regarding zinc supplements is that they can interact negatively with other medications. As such, it's important that you consult your doctor before beginning any new supplement, especially zinc.

Vitamin D supplements are another great option for controlling ADHD. Some recent research has shown that people with ADHD may be prone to lower levels of vitamin D than those without ADHD. There are no studies showing that vitamin D directly benefits ADHD, but I'd wager it can't hurt either. Getting your vitamin D levels tested or even taking a supplement is definitely not a bad idea, especially if you don't get much sunlight.

Besides, vitamin D has incredible benefits for the body, including strengthened muscles, bones, and immune system (Groth, 2022). This means that you or your child will be stronger and better equipped to fight off various illnesses by including more vitamin D in your life. Vitamin D is also phenomenal for oral health and the prevention of diabetes as well. Furthermore, taking a vitamin D supplement can help counteract hypertension associated with Adderall and similar medications, making it a phenomenal option for someone looking to take a combined approach to treatment. Beyond that, vitamin D is excellent for fighting depression, elevating the mood when you get more vitamin D in your system. For anyone with ADHD, I would absolutely recommend a vitamin D supplement.

Low levels of iron are another issue linked with ADHD, especially in children. It is known that iron is necessary for the brain to function, and some studies have shown that iron supplements can benefit ADHD symptoms. However, it's important to measure your level of iron before beginning supplementation, as too much iron can have negative impacts. Taking a chelated iron supplement is best to avoid digestive issues, and 30-40mg a day is usually a good starting dose of iron for adults. One of the many ways that iron improves brain function is by improving the ability of neurotransmitters to communicate, so it's no wonder that iron may be able to help prevent certain symptoms of ADHD.

There are many benefits to taking iron supplements. For one, this supplement is available in many forms, including pills and a liquid formula, allowing for it to be easily accessible to anyone, even if they can't swallow pills. This can be especially helpful for young children whose iron levels are lower than desirable. Furthermore, special forms of iron exist that can help prevent the stomach from getting upset upon taking iron, which is a common negative side effect that many people experience when they start taking iron. Additionally, it's very beneficial that iron is available in nearly any strength imaginable, making it perfectly personalizable to the needs of whoever is taking it. Outside of stomach issues, the only major drawback of oral iron supplements is that injections are absorbed better by the body; however, this isn't a major concern when it comes to iron as a treatment for ADHD. For these reasons, I definitely recommend consulting your doctor to see if an iron supplement is a good idea.

In addition, multivitamins have been particularly effective for children with ADHD, because it's important that kids with ADHD especially have sufficient levels of essential vitamins and minerals in order for the brain to function properly. Recent studies have shown that multivitamin supplements may be particularly effective in quelling some of the behavioral problems associated with ADHD as a result of their ability to infuse the body with any missing nutrients. Multivitamins may, therefore, benefit adults with behavioral or impulse control issues as well. The benefit of multivitamins is they're incredibly common, which means that they are both affordable and come in a myriad of different forms. This includes options for those with easily upset stomachs. Personally, I think multivitamins are a good option for anyone, depending on your specific body composition and vitamin deficiencies, so I think the benefits toward ADHD are just a fun added bonus to good health.

Finally, for the supplement category, we have magnesium. Magnesium is another excellent option for those with ADHD because it has noted abilities to calm hyperactive and agitated emotions. I would recommend anywhere from 100-300mg of magnesium to anyone who experiences rebound effects from their medication. It's important to avoid taking magnesium citrate by accident, though, as this product serves as a laxative.

As with the other supplements I've mentioned, there are various benefits and disadvantages to consider. One of the main benefits of magnesium supplements is that they are available over the counter, unlike all stimulant medications. They are accessible in many forms and dosages as well, which is perfect for various people. Furthermore, magnesium has many health benefits because it is one of the key nutrients that our bodies rely on. As far as negative impacts go, magnesium can cause stomach related issues like diarrhea or upset stomach, meaning that you should be careful when you first start taking it. Moreover, the effect of magnesium in children can be dangerous if not monitored closely, so be sure to consult your child's doctor before introducing this supplement to your child's diet.

If those options aren't up your alley, there are also therapeutic options for treatment that are available to you. One popular option that I mentioned briefly earlier is cognitive behavioral therapy, also known as CBT. CBT maintains the belief that distortions within our thoughts and emotions play a major part in how we act and navigate life (Raypole, 2021). This has to do with automatic thoughts we have in response to certain emotions, which can cause emotional distress and factor into various mental health disorders. When someone goes through CBT, they learn how to notice these thoughts and stop them in their tracks. Then, instead of allowing negative beliefs to take over, patients learn to think more realistic thoughts that don't hinder progress in life. Beyond that, CBT also equips people with relaxation techniques, problem solving skills, emotional regulation skills, and compassion and empathy-based lessons that allow for a more smooth and successful navigation of life.

As it turns out, CBT is particularly helpful for ADHD. CBT for ADHD focuses on learning skills which promote long-term change and growth in a way that medication cannot. CBT specifically for ADHD encourages skills surrounding organization, avoiding distractions, adaptive thinking, and the reduction of procrastination. In addition to that, psychoeducation is involved. This means that you would learn more about ADHD and how it impacts thought, as well as a thorough breakdown of how your therapeutic program would proceed. From there, you would begin to talk about the concerns that led you to seek therapy.

CBT has been incredibly effective in alleviating some of the common symptoms of ADHD, especially in adults. Multiple studies of the effects of CBT on teens and adults with ADHD modeled that CBT has the potential to improve ADHD symptoms that don't respond to medication. These studies also indicated that CBT was able to help alleviate associated anxiety, depression, and executive dysfunction felt by students with ADHD. A combination of medication and CBT seems to be the most effective for those with ADHD, however CBT alone can do far more than you think. In my personal experience, it's about a 70/30 mix, with 70% of the work being done in therapy and 30% being done by the medication. I truly think that CBT is an invaluable option for anyone seeking alternative, non-medication-based treatment for their ADHD.

Another option that many people with ADHD find to be particularly effective is mindfulness-based cognitive therapy. Mindfulness-based cognitive therapy is a form of therapy which combines meditation, cognitive behavioral therapy, and mindfulness in order to leave you with the most beneficial outcomes (Schimelpfening, 2021). Mindfulness itself involves focusing on the present and cultivating an attitude of non-judgment. There are various techniques employed within mindfulness-based cognitive therapy, including meditation, body scan exercises, mindfulness practices, stretching, and more. It has proved itself to be an incredibly effective technique at treating a wide range of mental health disorders, making it a valuable candidate for the treatment of ADHD. This practice also has various benefits to it, including allowing you to develop a more positive mindset and to confront your negative emotions.

Many studies have been conducted to verify the effectiveness of mindfulness-based cognitive therapy on ADHD. All of them seem to be incredibly hope-inspiring, allowing us to conclude that, perhaps, mindfulness-based cognitive therapy is a great option for those seeking a non-medicinal route to treat their ADHD.

For example, one study concluded that mindfulness meditation, a practice included in mindfulness-based cognitive therapy, has the potential to improve neural networks in the brain (Bachmann et al., 2016). This, in turn, leads to improvements in the brain for those with ADHD, directly benefiting the parts of the brain responsible for attention and emotional control. In other words, mindfulness meditation has proven to be beneficial at improving the levels of attention, focus, and impulsivity in those with ADHD. In another study, researchers determined that mindfulness-based cognitive therapy can be beneficial in a group format, and that in such a situation, it can be noticeably effective (Aadil et al., 2017). This has promising implications for group therapy, as it indicates that perhaps the implementation of mindfulness in group therapy benefits multiple participants at once, invigorating them with the benefits that mindfulness has to offer. This is something that I'm particularly interested in, as it seems especially promising. One final study I took note of concluded that mood and performance improved as a result of mindfulness-based cognitive therapy (Wozniak, 2022). This means that in correlation with ADHD treatment, mindfulness-based cognitive therapy has very effective, assuring impacts on those with behavioral and emotional issues as a result of their ADHD. Furthermore, this study also suggested that mindfulness-based cognitive therapy may be a suitable replacement for medication in some patients. Isn't that incredible?

From these studies, I can conclude that personally, I believe mindfulness-based cognitive therapy is a phenomenal solution for those with ADHD–whether they are seeking non-medicinal treatment or a combined approach. I feel confident in recommending this technique to anyone who has access to it, because it's incredibly beneficial. Besides inherently implementing CBT practices in its domain, this treatment option also uses mindfulness so effectively and permits use in a group setting. This means that there are opportunities for support and networking as well. If you're considering CBT but are unsure of its effectiveness, or you're looking for a therapeutic approach to ADHD treatment in general, then this is the option I'd recommend most.

A final option for therapy includes family therapy and couples counseling, depending on your particular circumstance. Family therapy has proven itself to be effective at lessening the impact of ADHD on a family, particularly families that have a child with ADHD (McQueen, n.d.). The main benefit of family therapy in these situations is that it allows your family to run more smoothly. It strengthens a sense of control, allows cohesion as a family unit, improves behavior, and models effective ways to work together as a family for the best results.

There is an option involved in family therapy called 'parent-directed treatment', which is obviously directed toward families with young children who have ADHD. Parent training is something involved in this option, and it allows for you to teach your child the skills they need. Parent-directed treatment is facilitated between a therapist and the parent, where the parent learns parenting skills that allow you to manage them more effectively. You'll learn skills like how to set boundaries and limits, improve organization, target specific behaviors and have appropriate consequences, turn mistakes into learning opportunities, and so much more. This is an option that I fully recommend to anyone with a child under the age of 12 who has ADHD.

Another family-based therapy option is integrated parent-child therapy, which occurs with children who are aged 8-18, depending. Parent-child therapy has many benefits, including improved parenting, decreased stress as a family, behavioral monitoring, and more effective discipline. This option is particularly effective for those with teenage children with ADHD, as it necessitates a deeper level of understanding from the child. This is another option I definitely recommend.

Marriage counseling or couples counseling is another type of therapy that can help alleviate some of the tumultuous issues caused by one partner having ADHD. In relationships where just one partner has ADHD, miscommunication and resentment can build up, creating conflict in the relationship. In couples counseling, the two of you learn how to meet relationship goals, develop communication strategies, and what changes can be put in place to address some of the biggest difficulties caused by ADHD. Additionally, you will garner a further understanding of how ADHD impacts you and your partner as a relationship unit. Most people experience stellar benefits as a result of attending couples counseling directed specifically toward those with ADHD. Some benefits couples have reported include accepting the individual role played in relationship difficulties, improved anger management, improved communication, elevated goal accomplishment, and more. If you're in a relationship with someone and experiencing significant difficulties, I recommend seeking out couples counseling specifically designed to address ADHD, as the benefits can make the difference between a successful marriage and a tiresome divorce.

Neurofeedback, also referred to as 'electroencephalograph (EEG) biofeedback', is another option for ADHD treatment. Neurofeedback is an analysis of brain waves that monitor the difference between our brain waves and their function throughout various stages of our consciousness or unconsciousness (Neurofeedback (EEG Biofeedback), n.d.). It has been incredibly effective at analyzing ADHD because EEG biofeedback has shown that those with ADHD experience significant differences in the waves that are active and inactive in the brain as compared to someone without ADHD. It is believed by some that the brain can be trained–or retrained–to experience "normal" brain waves, thus alleviating some of the most disturbing symptoms of ADHD. Using biofeedback as a potential option for treatment may work for some people who desire to treat their ADHD without medication, so do look into it if it sounds like something that would interest you.

Believe it or not, calming techniques have the power to influence us incredibly when it comes to our minds, and that's no different for the mind of someone with ADHD. Calming techniques are often recommended as a solution for many mental ailments, but many people also brush them off. How much can some breathing and yoga really do? As it turns out, a lot. Because one of the main issues people with ADHD experience is hyperactivity, calming exercises can be difficult, yet extremely beneficial. Fortunately, I have many tips pertaining to how you can make these calming exercises work for you, despite your ADHD, in order to then benefit your ADHD.

The first calming technique that I have in mind is meditation. Mindfulness meditation in particular is especially beneficial for those with ADHD because it improves our ability to pay attention (Levine, 2022). Within mindfulness meditation, you learn to observe yourself and focus. This helps with your prefrontal cortex, a part of the brain that controls planning, impulse control, and focus. Furthermore, mindfulness meditation helps raise the levels of dopamine in your brain, which is a chemical those with ADHD are notoriously low on. But meditating with ADHD can be hard.

The general image of meditation that comes to mind when you think about it is probably someone sitting cross-legged on the floor, being very still and silent. While this is a good tactic to take for meditation, it can be very ineffective and even frustrating for someone with ADHD. As such, there are some tips you can use to help you meditate more successfully without feeling like your ADHD is getting in the way. The first step to meditate with ADHD is to get comfortable. Don't force yourself into a position because you think it's right. Just get comfortable. Many people say that if you get too comfortable, you will likely fall asleep, but my philosophy is that if you fall asleep, then you needed the sleep anyway. So, find a comfortable position. Then, work your way toward taking slow and even breaths. You don't have to maintain any rhythm that's unnatural to you, and if you find yourself unable to do this, don't worry—your body will naturally soothe itself into a slower rate of breathing as you meditate anyway.

Another good idea to help you meditate if you have ADHD is to do something sensory-based that is the same every time you meditate. Lighting a specific scent of candle, sitting in the same place, or using a similar lighting every time you meditate will help trigger your senses to get into meditation mode when you need to calm down. Furthermore, it helps if you find something to focus your attention on. This can be a phrase or intention, or even music if that's something you want to try. When you find your mind wandering, gently and without judgment bring your attention back to whatever your focus for the meditation is.

Another tip, perhaps one of my favorites for meditating with ADHD, is to practice moving meditation. If while seated or lying you find yourself tempted to jitter or move around a lot, then try getting up and pacing, walking around, or engaging in some other rhythmic movement to ease that desire. Moving meditation is also effective and is better for people with ADHD usually. Remember, meditation is a state of mind, not a state of body.

I also recommend that you develop a meditation routine. Meditate at the same place and same time each day, and it'll slowly become much easier for you to do so. It can be hard to keep up a meditation routine, but there are some things that you should keep in mind. First, in my experience, it takes two to three weeks to see any major benefits of meditation, but once that time passes, it's all smooth sailing from there. If you're tempted to give up on your meditation practice after a few days, remind yourself of why you're doing it and challenge yourself to make it to the three-week mark before letting yourself give up. If after those three weeks you don't think meditation is doing for you what you expected it to, then you can move on and say that you tried.

It's also important that you avoid "should" statements in your practice. Don't force yourself to feel like you should do anything within your practice because you shouldn't. Do whatever you feel is best to help you achieve a successful meditation practice, whether or not that involves accommodations. Be kind to yourself and grant yourself the grace you need; forcing yourself to do something is very counterintuitive.

Deep breathing exercises can also be particularly soothing to those with ADHD and their minds, calming you down and providing you with the ability to focus. Deep breathing is known to benefit muscle tension, sleep, digestion, and stress, allowing for a full-body holistic benefit. A good, simple breathing exercise you can engage in is called 'square breathing'. You can square breathe with the following steps:

1. Pick a number from four to nine, which is going to be the number of seconds that you breathe.
2. Close your eyes and relax your body.
3. Imagine a square in your mind.
4. Inhale, and count to the number as you trace up one side of the square.
5. Hold your breath for the same number of seconds, tracing the top side of the square.
6. Exhale for the same number of seconds, letting yourself trace down the opposite side.

7. Pause for your number of seconds and trace the bottom.
8. Repeat until you feel soothed.

Another breathing exercise that I like and find particularly whimsical is called 'pufferfish breathing'. I like this exercise because it soothes the breath quickly and makes me smile a bit. Simply inhale as big as you can, allowing yourself to fill your body with air, visualizing yourself as a pufferfish. Notice how the air expands your lungs and stomach. Hold your breath for a few seconds before exhaling rapidly and all at once, like a pufferfish deflating. Repeat as needed.

Journaling can also make a world of difference for those with ADHD, but it can be hard to develop a stable journaling practice. How can journaling help with ADHD? There are a myriad of benefits of journaling for your ADHD (D., 2020). It can help you think more clearly and understand your feelings, for example. It may also help you learn to know yourself better and reduce levels of stress within you. Writing about how you feel can make you feel better, increasing your sense of calm and ability to remain focused on the present. Journaling also helps you solve problems more effectively, because writing allows us to use the creative aspects of our brain to solve logic-based problems. Beyond that, journaling can improve our ability to solve disagreements between ourselves and those around us. Writing about the ways we interact with others can allow us to see various perspectives of things, making sensible resolutions arise more quickly.

People with ADHD often struggle with starting and maintaining a journal because it goes into the ways in which people with ADHD struggle with executive functioning. Beyond that, up to half of people with ADHD have issues with written expression and writing in general, but even if writing is more difficult for you because of your ADHD, there are still things you can do to make the process of journaling easier. For example, finding the right journal is a crucial step (How ADHD Sufferers Can Learn to Journal Effectively, n.d.). You need to find one that fits your needs and working styles, but that can also be overwhelming. There are so many kinds of journals to choose from, so allow me to help you make the decision.

First, there are traditional journals that take place on paper with a pen. Think about your needs for a journal; do you want one that's lined, dotted, or blank? Do you want a journal that's portable or one that you can keep at home? This is important when considering the size of the journal. After that, you can decide if you want lined paper, dotted paper, or completely blank paper. You can also pick pens or pencils, even picking pens that are erasable to help you out. If that doesn't work for you, considering an electronic journal may. Electronic journals are great for their portability and convenience, and can often be an easier option for writing if you struggle with it. *Diarium* and *Momento* are two excellent apps that allow you to keep a journal daily.

If you've never journaled before, it can be complicated understanding how to start the journal. What do you even write in it? Well, there are a few strategies specifically for those with ADHD that make the process of journaling even easier. For starters, you can use the "brain dump" method to get your journal going, even when you're not sure what to write about. Simply write down everything you're thinking indiscriminately, and you've got yourself a brain dump. The benefit of brain dumping is that it allows you to see everything that's on your mind, as well as to evaluate the things that may be bothering you the most. This is particularly helpful when you don't know what to write about but feel compelled to write something. Another method you can use is a bullet journal, which combines aspects of planners with journaling. You can plan out your days and write about what you're going to do, and then reflect on what you actually did. You can also use a bullet journal to track emotions and habits as well.

Finally, you can journal based on prompts to have something to get you going.

If you work better from steps, here are some ADHD-friendly steps to get you going with the journaling process:

1. Develop a routine.
2. Decide on how much time you need to journal.
3. Be kind to yourself if you miss a day.
4. Be flexible with your plans to journal.
5. Journal in silence or with quiet music on to help you stay focused.

Another good calming method is to try physical activity for your ADHD. One of my personal favorites is yoga, because it has so many benefits. Yoga has many benefits, especially for people with ADHD (Martin, 2021). These benefits extend to lowering stress levels, making main easier to manage, improving mental health, reduced inattention, improved impulse control, and more. ADHD can be drastically improved by yoga because yoga activates parts of the brain that function less effectively in people with ADHD.

There are a few poses that are particularly good for people with ADHD. These poses include (Singh, 2022):

1. Cat-cow pose. Get down on your hands and knees, with your back flat and your hips aligned with your knees and shoulders with your wrists. Arch your back upwards, as if you would if you were imitating a black cat on Halloween. Then, let your back drop inwards and your head rise, as if you were imitating a cow. Go back and forth between these two poses, breathing steadily as you transition between the two.

2. Cobra pose. Lie down on your stomach and press your hands into the floor near where your shoulders are. Raise your upper body off the floor and look to the sky. Do this for a few breaths before moving to a different position.

You can also look up yoga videos for ADHD on YouTube to find the perfect yoga routine for you.

Finally, I want to talk to you about two more important factors that can benefit people with ADHD greatly–that is, sleep and time with nature. These are often suggested and twice as often ignored as options to improve mental health, but they're actually really good ways to improve upon the symptoms of disorders like ADHD.

Let's start with sleep. It can be hard to get to sleep when you have ADHD, or it can even be something you actively try to avoid, but the benefit of a good night's sleep cannot be overstated. This is because sleep has the ability to impair our cognitive function, which can make it even harder to pay attention (25 Tips, Tricks, and Tools to Get Sleep with ADHD – ADD Resource Center, 2020). That's no good for someone with ADHD, but fortunately, there are various tips which can assist in our ability to sleep better even with the interruptions presented by ADHD. These tips include:

- Sleeping in a comfortable but quiet room.
- Turn off your phone notifications. Do not disturb mode doesn't silence alarms, which means you can successfully sleep without hearing notifications but with your alarms on.
- Don't take your medication late in the day. Stimulant medications can last for a few hours, keeping you up if you take them too late.
- Don't take naps. Taking naps will make it harder to sleep at night.
- Try meditating.
- If you can't fall asleep, leave the bed. Tossing and turning in bed will build the association in your mind that the bed is for insomnia.

Outside of that, spending time with nature can be immensely helpful to those with ADHD. Spending time outdoors helps both the mind and body and can allow us to focus on something less demanding than day to day life. This can improve our short-term memory and provide us with a sense of calm unlike anything else, all from spending time with nature. Trust me, spending time outside is beneficial, even if you're spending time on your phone outside.

CHAPTER SUMMARY

- ADHD can be treated with supplements and vitamins, also known as natural remedies, if you have determined that medication is not for you.
- Ask yourself plenty of questions and carefully consider the side effects as well as the benefits before deciding if medication is for you.
- Things like calming techniques, EEG biofeedback, therapy, and supplements can help.

This chapter focused on teaching you all about "medicating" your ADHD with alternative treatment options. Now, you have so many tools to use for treating your ADHD without the use of prescription medication. From supplements to therapy, lifestyle changes to holistic treatments, there are so many things you can do that are incredibly effective for many people with ADHD. Try a combination of things and see what works for you. I genuinely believe that there are ways to improve your symptoms of ADHD, whether or not medication plays a role in your particular treatment plan. In the next chapter, we'll take a look at some of the ways people have benefitted from medication and non-medical treatment alike, giving you a more well-rounded perspective of the options available to you.

7

EFFECTIVE CASE STUDIES WITH MEDICATION AND WITHOUT

All our knowledge begins with the senses, proceeds then to the understanding, and ends with reason. There is nothing higher than reason. –Immanuel Kant

C ase studies are one of my favorite ways to garner knowledge about a new topic, especially when it comes to health. I think that there is so much we can learn from case studies, from observing the experiences of others and compiling them into opinions of our very own. So, of course, when it comes to ADHD treatment options–both medication and alternative treatments–I had to provide you with some case studies so that you could examine the successes of others for yourself. This chapter focuses on the stories and experiences of various people who have treated their ADHD in various ways, from medication to holistic and herbal treatments and more. I think that these case studies will provide you with a diverse, appreciative perspective regarding how experiences look across the board when it comes to ADHD treatment.

WITH MEDICATION

Many case studies exist supporting the fact that ADHD medications, like Adderall, make a striking difference in one's life. I find these case studies to be reassuring and informative, letting us know that even when medication can seem scary that people benefit heavily from taking the medication. So, here are several examples of people who say that their lives have been changed as a result of ADHD medication.

Below are some of the stories of people who tried ADHD medication and spoke on their experience on a website called *thrivingwithadhd.com* (Brown, 2018):

- "Medication has helped me turn my life around but it hasn't cured my condition." — Ren, 38. This is a very common statement made by many people who try ADHD medication. While it doesn't "cure" ADHD, it can certainly help alleviate some of the more negative effects associated with the condition.

- "It helps me to set goals, focus, problem solve and stay on track so I can complete tasks successfully." — Jo, 35. This is another common statement made by those who take medication for their ADHD. Medication has the power to allow us to focus and solve our problems in a more quick and effective manner than we could prior to taking medication.

- "It's only early days, but the diagnosis and medication has significantly helped me so far." — Chris, 43. This one is particularly moving to me. Even early on in his treatment, Chris was able to see some of the fantastic improvements associated with ADHD medication. This also speaks to me on another level; if ADHD medication isn't right for you, then you'll probably notice fairly quickly that it's not helping or even making your symptoms worse. This means that it's not going to be the case that you go years on a medication you shouldn't take–you'll know right away, and I think that's a really good thing.

- "I started taking Dextroamphetamine, and after I got the dosage right, I noticed amazing improvements." — Rachel. Rachel's story really emphasizes one of the main reasons why taking medication by being monitored by a doctor is important. Getting dosages correct can be rather tricky, but once you've got them down, your life will be exhilarated with benefit.

- "...the medication has really helped me get back on track and I can now complete my duties without exhausting myself." — Michael, 33. Something not too many people talk about is how exhausting living with ADHD can be. Forcing yourself to function "normally" within a society not built with your needs in mind can be exhausting. Fortunately, with the power of ADHD medication, that doesn't have to be the case.

- "Taking medication has been life changing." — Kendra, 31. I think this one speaks for itself.

- "I am on medication now for my ADHD and put simply, I could not function without it." — Clinton, 37. In light of the Adderall shortage in the United States, I think it's so important to keep this in mind when it comes to making sure that people can get their medications.

There are so many other, similar stories as well that highlight the life changing improvements that can be made when taking ADHD medication. For example, Elan, age 44, was initially seeing a doctor for depression and struggled immensely (Abramson, 2022). He asked his doctor if it was possible that he could have ADHD, to which his doctor said it was possible. After starting Adderall, his life changed, but he went off his medication again shortly after. Once he got back on his medication, he realized that this is something he'll probably be taking for life, and he's not ashamed of it. He says doing work around the house and for his job is much less challenging, and that's an improvement I love to see.

Lauren, 27, had similar experiences with her ADHD medication. She was originally diagnosed with depression and prescribed Zoloft, which helped with her mood but not her attention. In recent years, she realized that she might have ADHD and began taking Concerta and Ritalin. After that, it felt like a cloud lifted; she could focus better, organize her thoughts, communicate better, and so much more. Lauren plans to remain on her medication indefinitely because of the benefits it's had for her.

These stories go to show that ADHD medication has the power to truly change one's life, but don't feel like you have to take medication just because of me or these stories, though; next, we'll talk about alternative treatments that can be used for ADHD.

ALTERNATIVE TREATMENT

In addition, there are so many case studies showing that alternative treatments have made a world of difference for those with ADHD. This section will focus on all of those case studies, allowing you to see how successful your ADHD treatment can be without medication–hopefully alleviating any pressure you feel about the situation.

According to Medium writer Scott Wilkinson, he had the ability to lead a successful life with ADHD without the influence of medication. His experiences with ADHD started as young as age seven, where Wilkinson was prone to disturbing classmates and teachers alike with distracting behaviors (Wilkinson, 2016). Drumming, believe it or not, is one of the things that changed his life. He developed a passion for music and then became obsessed with drumming due to the meditative state that repetition has to offer. In fact, he attended Juilliard for his music skills as a result of his music passion. Now, let me be transparent, Wilkinson did try various ADHD medications all to no avail, but ultimately, it was lifestyle changes that led to his success.

Thousands of other people have been able to manage their ADHD without medication, and as such, I'll list several of them below, based on methods and changes that truly altered the course of various people's lives:

CBT

- Major benefits from CBT were experienced by many people, allowing for transformations in people's lives.
- When combined with medication, CBT was even more effective.
- The biggest thing people talk about in correlation with CBT for ADHD is that stopping their therapy caused major issues with their symptoms reappearing. Therefore, my recommendation is that you remain in therapy until your therapist indicates that you're ready to move on.

Biofeedback

- Various participants in biofeedback related ADHD treatment had the experience that not only did it help, but over time, the improvements were sustained and heightened.

Meditation

- Parents of children who participated in mindfulness and meditation studies experienced stellar effects as well when interviewed. Parents described that they were able to spend more time with their child, support their child better, and overall had an improved family experience.
- Children who participated in meditative and mindfulness training also felt seen and heard by spending time with other kids like themselves.
- Furthermore, mindfulness provokes focus and non-judgment of thoughts, which is thought to be especially helpful for children with ADHD. Instead of viewing distracting thoughts as bad or negative, mindfulness teaches that they're just thoughts and shouldn't be condemned. This, in turn, allows for less distress surrounding an ADHD mentality.

Other successful treatment options and changes that aren't medication

- Coping strategies, such as noise-canceling earbuds and headphones, making a space impulse friendly, meditation, focusing on small goals, and practicing radical self-acceptance, have helped people transform their lives.
- Intensive exercise has been beneficial for people with severe mood and motivation issues.
- Caffeine taken in small doses throughout the day, alongside omega-3 supplements, benefited people as well, removing some of the brain fog as well as eliminating a lack of concentration and focus.
- Many people experience benefits from routine and implementing moderate exercise into their routine as well.
- Yoga early in the morning was beneficial to focus and concentration.
- Restricting and avoiding distractions during work times also helped people out.
- Sleeping well and keeping consistent wake and sleep times assisted in eliminating some of the side effects of ADHD.
- Using memory aids helped prevent memory-based issues and distractions. For example,

using phone reminders and alarms was particularly beneficial.

- Taking breaks with timers to remind you to continue to work can also help.
- Having something quiet to fidget with helps with focus.
- Putting things you often forget in places you need them or really noticeable locations can prevent forgetting the things you need.
- Organizing tasks into a planner was helpful for many people.
- Eating regularly and avoiding foods that make you tired can provide an energy boost.
- Using apps and browser extensions helps with work for many who have ADHD.

CHAPTER SUMMARY

- Adderall has been incredibly effective in a wide variety of case studies, as have been other remedies for ADHD.

Case studies are, as I mentioned, one of my favorite ways to learn from the experiences of others. They show us what others went through and provide the details of how, allowing for us to compile our own opinions based off of them. After hearing about the examples of people who improved their ADHD—both with and without medication—I am confident that you know which choice you will want to make. In the next chapter, I'm going to provide you with some final resources that allow for you to know who to turn to for continued support after this book.

8

RECOMMENDATIONS BEYOND THIS BOOK

The point of modern propaganda is not only to misinform or push an agenda. It is to exhaust your critical thinking, to annihilate truth. —Garry Kasparov

The myths that surround ADHD and medication are so endlessly harmful. Thousands of people miss out on life changing treatment as a result of common myths that perpetuate a harmful stigma about ADHD, treatments, and those who have it. Myths regarding where ADHD comes from–bad parenting, vaccines, only in boys–prevent so many people from getting the diagnoses that they deserve (Posner, 2006). Beyond that, myths that ADHD was created just to make money off of those who need medication are not only wildly inappropriate but prevent people from the treatment they rightfully deserve as well. The importance of accurate information is invaluable in our society; everyone deserves the right to receive all of the resources that they need to survive and thrive. As such, this chapter is dedicated to providing you with resources outside of this book to allow you to continue with your journey in healing, recovering, and living the life you truly deserve.

FINDING A DOCTOR

Finding a reliable, good doctor to diagnose your ADHD and/or prescribe you medication is necessary for your safety. In adults, there are many people who can diagnose ADHD. Those people include psychologists, psychiatrists, and neurologists. These are the only people who I would recommend seeking out to receive your ADHD diagnoses. Furthermore, you should only receive a prescription from a psychiatrist, neurologist, or physician with the capacity to prescribe stimulant medication.

If you have never had to look for a specialized doctor before, it can be confusing and daunting to know how to weed out the good doctors from the perfect doctors.

Because of this, I have a handful of questions that you can ask potential candidates, including (Novotni, 2015):

1. How many clients have you treated for ADHD specifically?
2. How long has your practice involved working with adults who have ADHD?
3. How do you assess and treat ADHD within your particular practice?
4. Have you received special training that revolves around adult ADHD?
5. What are the costs I can anticipate if I opt to work with you?

These questions will allow you to better gauge the doctor's experience personally with clients who are adults and have ADHD, as well as allow you to understand if their particular methods of treatment are in line with your desired treatment options.

In addition, you might find yourself in search of an ADHD clinic to especially attend to your needs. As such, I have compiled multiple lists of ADHD clinics you can visit regionally throughout the United States.

Northeast:

- The Sachs Center. Visit *sachscenter.com* or dial (646) 603-0491.

Mid-Atlantic:

- Center for Neurocognitive Excellence. Visit *www.adhd-center-dc.com* or call 202-998-ADHD.
- Kennedy Krieger Institute. Visit *www.kennedykrieger.org/behavioralpsych* or call 443-923-7508.

Midwest:

- ADHD Centers Chicago. Visit *www.addcenters.com.*
- The ADHD Center of Milwaukee. Visit *ADHDcom.org* or call 312-375-3170.

West:

- Millennium Medical Associates. Call 310-460-5917 or visit *www.millenniummedicalassociates.com.*

- ReFocus ADHD. Visit www.refocusadhdutah.com or call 801-410-0070.

Southwest:

- ADD/ADHD Diagnostic & Treatment Center. Visit *docyoung.com* or call 972-943-0410.

APPS FOR ADHD

In a world where technology surrounds us at every turn, employing the powerful benefits it has to offer can change our lives greatly. For those with ADHD, there are so many apps available that you can try to make your life simpler. I have organized these apps into a list based on their purpose so that you can quickly sort out the perfect apps for you:

- Focus: *Forest, Brain Focus*
- Note taking: *Evernote*
- Homework/Studying: *Trello, Quizlet, Khan Academy*
- Reading: *Beeline Reader*
- White noise: *Noisli*
- Self-care: *Calm, Headspace*

WEBSITES AND LEARNING MATERIALS

Finally, the following list contains various resources for learning more about ADHD.

- Attention Deficit Disorder Association
- Children and Adults with Attention-Deficit/Hyperactivity Disorder
- Mental Health America
- National Alliance on Mental Illness
- National Federation of Families for Children's Mental Health
- National Institute of Mental Health
- National Institute of Mental Health ADHD
- National Resource Center on ADHD
- CHADD
- ADDitude
- ADD.org
- Understood.org

This chapter focused on providing you with resources that help you know where to go after reading this book. This is the eighth and final chapter, and I want to congratulate you for learning about ADHD medication and other treatments. You now have such a solid, strong understanding of ADHD and everything associated with it, from similar medications to side effects and how to avoid addiction. You are ready to pave your better future using the lessons you've learned from this book. Keep reading on for a final note!

CONCLUSION

Welcome to the end of our journey together; at least, for now. This book has taught you nearly everything there is to know about Adderall and how to use it properly. Now, you know the difference between Adderall and other similar ADHD medications. You also know how to take Adderall properly vs. improperly, about all of the potential side effects that can accompany taking Adderall, and the dangers of black-market usage of Adderall. Beyond that, you have learned some valuable information about alternative resources and treatment options for ADHD.

Overall, it is important to understand that Adderall is not a bad medication, but there are bad ways to use it. Adderall has been incredibly helpful to many people, transforming their lives entirely. While medication is super helpful, you do need to be wary of the potential side effects. Now, you have one of the best resources around to reference regarding Adderall and safety concerns. It is time for you to let your worries float away, medicate without anxiety, and live happily.

If you found this book to be valuable or educational, please consider leaving a review on Amazon. That way, others with the same worries as you can find this valuable resource. Trust me, it may not seem like a lot to just leave a review for something, but finding this book can change the lives of those just like you if only they can access it.

Finally, I want to end the book on a more personal note. Thank you for entrusting me to teach you all I know about Adderall and other ADHD medications. I was once in your position too—lacking confidence and trust in medication options available to me—but I'm endlessly grateful for the learning opportunities that led me to the confidence in Adderall that I have today. I hope you can one day meet me here, from a place of success and satisfaction with your own ADHD treatment.

Good luck on your journey from here. Use what you have learned to effectively treat your ADHD and live the suffering-free life you deserve!

REFERENCES

25 Tips, Tricks, and Tools To Get Sleep with ADHD – ADD Resource Center. (2020). https://www.addrc.org/25-tips-tricks-and-tools-to-get-sleep-with-adhd/

Aadil, M., Cosme, R. M., & Chernaik, J. (2017). Mindfulness-Based Cognitive Behavioral Therapy as an Adjunct Treatment of Attention Deficit Hyperactivity Disorder in Young Adults: A Literature Review. *Cureus*, *9*(5). https://doi.org/10.7759/cureus.1269

Abramson, A. (2022, September 16). *ADHD Medication: What It's Like To Take Adderall And Other Meds For ADHD.* The Paper Gown. https://www.zocdoc.com/blog/4-people-on-taking-adhd-meds/

Adderall & Psychosis, Paranoia | How Does Adderall Affect People with Psychosis? (2022). The Recovery Village Drug and Alcohol Rehab. https://www.therecoveryvillage.com/adderall-addiction/adderall-causes-psychosis-schizophrenia/

Adderall Addiction Aftercare and Relapse Prevention. (n.d.). https://www.mentalhelp.net/substance-abuse/adderall/aftercare/

Adderall Addiction Treatment. (n.d.). Footprints to Recovery | Drug Rehab & Alcohol Addiction Treatment Centers. Retrieved April 14, 2023, from https://footprintstorecovery.com/adderall-addiction/

Adderall for ADHD/ADD: Uses, Dosages, Side Effects, Treatment. (2022). Www.additudemag.com. https://www.additudemag.com/adderall-adhd-medication-faq/

Adderall XR Oral: Uses, Side Effects, Interactions, Pictures, Warnings & Dosing - WebMD. (n.d.). Www.webmd.com. Retrieved April 14, 2023, from https://www.webmd.com/drugs/2/drug-63164/adderall-xr-oral/details#:~:text=Loss%20of%20appetite%2C%20weight%20loss

ADHD: to medicate or not to medicate? (2021, July 15). The ADHD Centre.

https://www.adhdcentre.co.uk/adhd-to-medicate-or-not-to-medicate/

American Academy of Pediatrics. (2019, September 27). *Causes of ADHD: What We Know Today*. HealthyChildren.org. https://www.healthychildren.org/English/health-issues/conditions/adhd/Pages/Causes-of-ADHD.aspx

Bachmann, K., Lam, A. P., & Philipsen, A. (2016). Mindfulness-Based Cognitive Therapy and the Adult ADHD Brain: A Neuropsychotherapeutic Perspective. *Frontiers in Psychiatry*, 7(117). https://doi.org/10.3389/fpsyt.2016.00117

Bhandari, S. (2021, March 8). *Stimulant Medications for ADHD*. WebMD. https://www.webmd.com/add-adhd/adhd-stimulant-therapy

Bhargava, H. (2008, August 27). *ADHD Medications and Side Effects*. WebMD; WebMD. https://www.webmd.com/add-adhd/adhd-medication-chart

Broadbent, E. (2021). *Adderall for Adults? Yes! How Treating My ADHD Changed My Life*. Www.additudemag.com. https://www.additudemag.com/eureka-adhd-meds-gave-me-a-whole-new-life/

Brown, L. (2018, July 9). *You Are Not Alone: Adults with ADHD Share Their Stories*. Thriving with ADHD. https://thrivingwithadhd.com.au/blog/you-are-not-alone-adults-with-adhd-share-their-stories/

Center, A. G. (2022, April 5). *Why Can't I Get Refills On My Stimulant? (and other related questions)*. Afg Guidance Center. https://afgfamily.com/blog/adhd/why-cant-i-get-refills-on-my-stimulant-and-other-related-questions/

Centers for Disease Control and Prevention. (2021, September 23). *Data and statistics about ADHD*. Centers for Disease Control and Prevention. https://www.cdc.gov/ncbddd/adhd/data.html

Centers for Disease Control and Prevention. (2022, August 9). *What Is ADHD?* Centers for Disease Control and Prevention. https://www.cdc.gov/ncbddd/adhd/facts.html

Cleveland Clinic. (2022, October 6). *ADHD Medications: How They Work & Side Effects*. Cleveland Clinic. https://my.clevelandclinic.org/health/treatments/11766-adhd-medication

Cristol, H. (2022). *Side Effects of Adderall*. WebMD. https://www.webmd.com/add-adhd/adderall-side-effects

D., J. (2020). *Benefits of Journal Writing for Adults with ADHD*. Www.additudemag.com. https://www.additudemag.com/benefits-of-journal-writing-for-adults-with-adhd/

Drugs & Medications. (2019). Webmd.com. https://www.webmd.com/drugs/2/drug-148324/vyvanse-oral/details

Drugs.com. (2017). *Adderall*. Drugs.com; Drugs.com. https://www.drugs.com/adderall.html

drugs.com. (2019). *Concerta*. Drugs.com; Drugs.com. https://www.drugs.com/concerta.html

End Adderall Cravings, Prevent Relapse and Find Help. (n.d.). Recovery.org. https://recovery.org/adderall/cravings/

Focalin Oral: Uses, Side Effects, Interactions, Pictures, Warnings & Dosing - WebMD. (n.d.). Www.webmd.com. https://www.webmd.com/drugs/2/drug-22256/focalin-oral/details

Geoffrion, L. (2023). *Adderall Effects, Risks, and Dangers: Short and Long Term*. American Addiction Centers. https://americanaddictioncenters.org/adderall/long-term-effects#:~:text=In%20fact%2C%20in%202020%2C%205.1

Gordon, J. (2015, January 28). *Ask the Expert: Raynaud's Phenomenon -*. HSS Playbook Blog. https://www.hss.edu/playbook/ask-the-expert-raynauds-phenomenon/

Gorman, J. (2022, November 28). *Adderall Addiction Vs Adderall Dependence: A Complete Guide | Asheville Recovery Center*. https://www.ashevillerecoverycenter.com/adderall-addiction-vs-adderall-dependence/

Groth, L. (2022). *9 Vitamin D Benefits You Should Know—and How to Get More in Your Diet*. Health.com. https://www.health.com/nutrition/vitamins-supplements/vitamin-d-benefits

Hobbs, H. (2014, August 20). *The Effects of Adderall on Your Body*. Healthline. https://www.healthline.com/health/adhd/adderall-effects-on-body#Central-nervous-system

How ADHD Sufferers Can Learn to Journal Effectively. (n.d.). JournalOwl.

Retrieved April 15, 2023, from https://www.journalowl.com/blog/how-adhd-sufferers-can-learn-to-journal-effectively

How To Get Prescribed Adderall For ADHD Online | Klarity. (2022, February 23). Www.klarityadhd.com. https://www.klarityadhd.com/post/adderall-for-adhd/

Hritani, A., Minocha, V., Patel, A., & Antoun, P. (2015). Adderall XR and peripheral arterial vasculopathy: A case report and a review of the literature. *Reviews in Vascular Medicine*, *3*(1), 1–4. https://doi.org/10.1016/j.rvm.2015.03.001

ILikePotatoesNotYams. (2020, June 15). *What's your Adderall success story?* Reddit. https://www.reddit.com/r/adderall/comments/h9mz8g/whats_your_adderall_success_story/

Johnston, H. (2019, October 11). *Mother-of-two reveals addiction to Adderall ruined her life*. Mail Online. https://www.dailymail.co.uk/femail/article-7562085/Mother-two-reveals-addiction-Adderall-ruined-life-robbed-years-children.html

Kashyap, N. (2022). *Can Adderall Increase Anger and Irritability?* Verywell Health. https://www.verywellhealth.com/adderall-irritability-and-anger-5714739

Kennedy, M. (2020). *How Adderall works and how it helps ADHD*. Insider. https://www.insider.com/guides/health/mental-health/what-does-adderall-do

Knibbs, K. (2022, October 26). *America's Adderall Shortage Could Kill People*. Wired. https://www.wired.com/story/adderall-shortage-problems/

Levine, H. (2022, January 17). *Meditation and Yoga for ADHD*. WebMD. https://www.webmd.com/add-adhd/adhd-mindfulness-meditation-yoga

Liao, S. (n.d.). *Why Are ADHD Medicines Controlled Substances?* WebMD. https://www.webmd.com/add-adhd/features/adhd-medicines-controlled-substances

Llamas, M. (2023). *Adderall Side Effects | Common, Serious and Long-Term Effects*. Drugwatch.com. https://www.drugwatch.com/adderall/side-effects/

Martin, L. (2021, September 30). *Yoga for people with ADHD: Benefits, what to know, and more.* Www.medicalnewstoday.com. https://www.medical newstoday.com/articles/adhd-yoga#does-it-reduce-symptoms

Mcilvena, L. (2022, October 3). *Is Self-Prescribing Legal?* GoodRx; GoodRx. https://www.goodrx.com/hcp/providers/self-prescrib ing-laws-by-state#:~:text=Prescribing%20any%20scheduled% 20medication%20for

McQueen, J. (n.d.). *Family Therapy for Childhood ADHD: What to Know.* WebMD. https://www.webmd.com/add-adhd/childhood-adhd/ childhood-adhd-family-therapy

Medicines and side effects. (2012). Vic.gov.au. https://www.betterhealth. vic.gov.au/health/conditionsandtreatments/ medicines-and-side-effects

Nall, R. (2019, June 4). *Does Adderall Make You Poop? How It Affects Your Digestive System.* Healthline. https://www.healthline.com/health/ does-adderall-make-you-poop-2#effect-on-digestion

Neurofeedback (EEG Biofeedback). (n.d.). CHADD. https://chadd.org/ about-adhd/neurofeedback-eeg-biofeedback/

Newmark, S. (2019, February 6). *10 ADHD Supplements and Vitamins for Symptom Control.* ADDitude. https://www.additudemag.com/vita mins-minerals-adhd-treatment-plan/

Novotni, M. (2015, January 29). *Choosing a Professional to Diagnose and Treat ADHD.* ADDitude; ADDitude. https://www.additudemag. com/self-diagnosis-adhd-how-to-find-professional/

Patterson, E. (2022). *How to Recognize an Adderall Overdose.* https:// www.goodrx.com/adderall/adderall-overdose

Patterson, E. (2023). *Adderall Abuse | Signs, Symptoms and Addiction Treatment.* DrugAbuse.com. https://drugabuse.com/stimulants/ adderall/

Pearson, K. (2017, December 5). *How Omega-3 Fish Oil Affects Your Brain and Mental Health.* Healthline. https://www.healthline.com/nutri tion/omega-3-fish-oil-for-brain-health#TOC_TITLE_HDR_3

Pera, G. (2022, September 1). *How Can Medication Help ADHD Relationships?* ADHD Roller Coaster — Gina Pera. https://

adhdrollercoaster.org/book-club/how-can-medication-help-adhd-relationships/

Posner, J. (2006, October 6). *9 ADHD Myths and Fallacies That Perpetuate Stigma*. ADDitude. https://www.additudemag.com/adhd-myths-and-facts-learn-the-truth-about-attention-deficit/

Raypole, C. (2021, October 7). *How Cognitive Behavioral Therapy Can Help Manage ADHD*. Healthline. https://www.healthline.com/health/adhd/cbt-for-adhd#what-it-is

Reale, Z. (2022). *How to Get Prescribed Adderall: Everything You Need to Know*. Choosing Therapy. https://www.choosingtherapy.com/how-to-get-prescribed-adderall/

Recovery, C. W. C. (2022, March 29). *Adderall: The Infamous Study Drug*. Comprehensive Wellness Centers. https://www.cwcrecovery.com/blog/adderall-the-infamous-study-drug/

Ritalin Oral: Uses, Side Effects, Interactions, Pictures, Warnings & Dosing - WebMD. (n.d.). Www.webmd.com. https://www.webmd.com/drugs/2/drug-9475/ritalin-oral/details#:~:text=This%20medication%20is%20used%20to

Rodden, J. (2019, June 26). *ADHD Medication Rebound: What to Do When a Prescription Wears Off*. ADDitude. https://www.additudemag.com/adhd-medication-rebound/#:~:text=ADHD%20medication%20rebound%2C%20sometimes%20called

Schimelpfening, N. (2021, July 14). *How Mindfulness-Based Cognitive Therapy Works*. Verywell Mind. https://www.verywellmind.com/mindfulness-based-cognitive-therapy-1067396

Serotonin Syndrome – Adderall and Serotonin. (2018, March 28). The Recovery Village Drug and Alcohol Rehab. https://www.therecoveryvillage.com/adderall-addiction/serotonin-syndrome-adderall/

Singh, M. (2022). *ADHD: 4 Yoga Asanas For People With ADHD*. NDTV.com. https://www.ndtv.com/health/adhd-4-yoga-asanas-for-people-with-adhd-3109287

Study Drug Facts, History and Statistics | Dangers and Legality. (2023). DrugAbuse.com. https://drugabuse.com/stimulants/adderall/history-and-statistics-of-study-drugs/

The Medical Info on How Adderall Impacts Your Sex Drive. (n.d.).

Www.blueheart.io. https://www.blueheart.io/post/the-medical-info-on-how-adderall-impacts-your-sex-drive

WebMD. (2016, August 29). *Potential Side Effects of ADHD Medicine.* WebMD; WebMD. https://www.webmd.com/add-adhd/child hood-adhd/adhd-common-side-effects-children

What are side effects and why do they occur? | Guides | HIV i-Base. (n.d.). I-Base.info. https://i-base.info/guides/side/what-are-side-effects#:~: text=Why%20do%20side%20effects%20occur

What Does Adderall Do to Your Brain? It Depends | Caron. (n.d.). Caron Treatment Centers. https://www.caron.org/blog/what-does-adder all-do-to-your-brain-it-depends

Where Families Find Answers on Substance Use | Partnership for Drug-Free Kids. (2017). Where Families Find Answers on Substance Use | Partnership for Drug-Free Kids. https://drugfree.org/

Why Your Pharmacist Can't Fill Your Prescription — and What To Do About It. (n.d.). GoodRx. https://www.goodrx.com/healthcare-access/ pharmacies/why-pharmacist-wont-fill-prescription-what-you-can-do

Wilkinson, S. (2016, October 1). *A Successful Life With ADHD—Without Drugs.* Renaissance Life. https://medium.com/renaissance-life/a-successful-life-with-adhd-without-drugs-2da91360ed1f

Wozniak, J. (2022). Mindfulness-Based Cognitive Therapy (MBCT) and ADHD Undergraduate Students : A Commentary On Randomized Controlled Trial Results. *Intersect: The Stanford Journal of Science, Technology, and Society, 15*(2). https://ojs.stanford.edu/ojs/ index.php/intersect/article/view/2035

www.ingramcontent.com/pod-product-compliance
Lightning Source LLC
Chambersburg PA
CBHW070709130626
46553CB00005B/1903